ROUTLEDGE LIBRARY EDITIONS BROADCASTING

Volume 35

TELEVISION

TELEVISION

A Critical Review

GERALD BEADLE

Routledge
Taylor & Francis Group

LONDON AND NEW YORK

First published in 1963 by George Allen & Unwin Ltd

This edition first published in 2024
by Routledge
4 Park Square, Milton Park, Abingdon, Oxon OX14 4RN

and by Routledge
605 Third Avenue, New York, NY 10158

Routledge is an imprint of the Taylor & Francis Group, an informa business

© 1963 George Allen & Unwin Ltd

All rights reserved. No part of this book may be reprinted or reproduced or utilised in any form or by any electronic, mechanical, or other means, now known or hereafter invented, including photocopying and recording, or in any information storage or retrieval system, without permission in writing from the publishers.

Trademark notice: Product or corporate names may be trademarks or registered trademarks, and are used only for identification and explanation without intent to infringe.

British Library Cataloguing in Publication Data
A catalogue record for this book is available from the British Library

ISBN: 978-1-032-59391-3 (Set)
ISBN: 978-1-032-61993-4 (Volume 35) (hbk)
ISBN: 978-1-032-61995-8 (Volume 35) (pbk)
ISBN: 978-1-032-61994-1 (Volume 35) (ebk)

DOI: 10.4324/9781032619941

Publisher's Note
The publisher has gone to great lengths to ensure the quality of this reprint but points out that some imperfections in the original copies may be apparent.

Disclaimer
The publisher has made every effort to trace copyright holders and would welcome correspondence from those they have been unable to trace.

(photo: BBC)

Television
A Critical Review

GERALD BEADLE

London
GEORGE ALLEN & UNWIN LTD
RUSKIN HOUSE MUSEUM STREET

FIRST PUBLISHED IN 1963

This book is copyright under the Berne Convention. Apart from any fair dealing for the purpose of private study, research, criticism or review, as permitted under the Copyright Act, 1956, no portion may be reproduced by any process without written permission. Enquiries should be addressed to the publisher.

© *George Allen & Unwin Ltd.*, 1963

PRINTED IN GREAT BRITAIN
in 11 point Juliana type
BY EAST MIDLAND PRINTING CO. LTD
BURY ST. EDMUNDS

CONTENTS

1. I Join the BBC — page 9
2. Life in the BBC — 15
3. The Birth of Public Television — 38
4. Who Controls Television? — 43
5. Money — 55
6. The Liberty of British Television — 64
7. Monopoly and Competition — 70
8. Television and Advertising — 81
9. Education and Instruction — 93
10. Global Television — 107
11. Canned Television — 119
12. Colour Television — 131
13. Pay TV — 137
14. Into the Future — 145

INDEX — 151

CHAPTER 1

I Join the BBC

In June, 1961, I came to the end of thirty-eight years as a broadcaster, thirty-six of those years in the service of the BBC, and I have recently been asking myself what qualifications, if any, I had for such a career. A high proportion of the BBC staff were born into families involved in some way in human communications; teachers, authors, composers, journalists, clergy, actors, musicians and politicians all belong to the communicating class, and it is natural for children brought up in such environments to accept public communication as a normal activity for educated persons. In 1922 broadcasting, though new, was just another medium of communication, and those born to the notion of communication had no difficulty in adopting it and making it their own.

But the atmosphere surrounding me in childhood was very different. Communicators as a race were not held in particularly high regard in my family; they were tolerated as persons who sometimes rendered useful services to society, and if they had outstanding talent they were admired; but as a class their status was relatively low. They operated on the fringes, constructively or mischievously as the case may be, but they stood outside the main business of life, which was to make good things and to sell them. Industry, agriculture, trade and transport were of the first importance and the people who pursued these occupations were the important people, because they contributed to the real wealth of the community.

Apart from my parents, the dominant personalities in my early years were my two grandfathers, Charles Beadle and Andrew Pears; both in their way distinguished men. Though temperamentally very different they had much in common; both made a lot of money by the standards of those days; neither was content with one house, each needed three; one owned Woodhall at Arkesden in Essex, the other The Wakes at Selborne in Hampshire. Neither was content with the size of his country house and both added large wings to accommodate billiard rooms, extra bedrooms and bathrooms. (Both houses have recently been restored to their original and more beautiful state by the complete demolition of my grandfathers' excrescences.) Both had such things as motor cars and electric light when they were in their infancy, and one of them, Charles Beadle, was an inveterate sailor. When he and his skipper, Bob Holloway, got too old to sail he bought a hundred-ton steam yacht, and kept it till they were too old even for that. Both grandfathers were addicted to field sports, especially shooting, and pheasants were reared in large numbers.

Andrew Pears had inherited the family business of A. and F. Pears, soapmakers, which had been founded by his great-grandfather in the eighteenth century, and at the time of his death in 1910 he was described by the press as the originator and first practitioner of modern mass advertising. I was eleven when he died.

Charles Beadle played a much bigger direct part in my life, because he remained in excellent health till his death at the age of ninety-three, when I was twenty-six. He outlived my father by eight years; indeed he outlived his wife and most of his children. He had been an importer of seaborne coal mainly from Tyneside, having established his own wharf at Erith in the mid-nineteenth century, because he foresaw that the growing size of steamships would make the deeper waters of the Thames estuary more attractive and profitable for shipping. He played a big part in the development of steam power for industry, especially paper-making, and he was one of the leading figures in the gas industry in London. He retired with a fortune when he was sixty, and lived for another thirty-three years to enjoy it.

These two successful and forceful characters set the tone of the two families into which I was born in 1899, when they were at the peak of their success. Because they were both extroverts and immensely hospitable to their large families, I was able to partake of the fruits of wealth at a very early age, and to get to know my numerous relations uncommonly well. As I was the eldest of a large litter, my mother was only too pleased to send me to my grandparents whenever she could, which suited me admirably at the time, though it may have given me extravagant tastes which I sometimes found it difficult to live up to in later years.

My father was a consulting chemist in private practice. Most industries today have their own research departments, but at the beginning of the century it was not so, and there was great scope for the independent professional research worker. As junior partner in Cross, Bevan and Beadle he invented what came to be known as Rayon, and sold the process to Courtaulds the silk weavers; later, as senior partner in Clayton Beadle and Stevens, he developed many other industrial processes, especially in paper making, rubber and road surfacing. At forty-six he got cancer and died at forty-nine, when I was eighteen and just about to leave school; life did not give him time completely to fulfil himself. He was the happiest man I ever knew and the most lovable; if there was any fun to be had Father was always in the middle of it. His chief recreation was fox hunting, and he often took me with him. From him I learnt many things—most of all the infectious nature of happiness, especially in the head of a family.

Such was the fecundity of my parents that they produced six children in eight years, of which I was the eldest, and next to me came three sisters. My mother employed a head nurse and an under-nurse, and so I was a single slice of masculinity in the middle of large female sandwich. This situation gave me a hierarchical sense and an understanding of the balance of power. The head nurse, being the chief disciplinarian, was not often on my side, while my eldest sister was inevitably the chief rival for power in the nursery, and at quite an early stage I discovered how profitable it was in such circumstances to form an alliance with the under-nurse and my second sister. With their loyal support, which I often did not deserve, I managed to maintain the traditional supremacy of the male. It was a happy home for young children, and I have always been glad that I was a day boy at a preparatory school until I was thirteen, because it kept me as a full resident member of the family for long enough to learn how families work.

The influences of the total environment were clear cut and simple. There was a strong traditional sense of right and wrong which was not very obviously equated with Christianity; it seemed rather to be indigenous to the family; but Christianity of the Anglican variety was something we all accepted, albeit with a few pinches of salt here and there. Divorce was ungentlemanly, not so much because God disapproved of it, but because the Beadles disapproved of it; it was a kind of failure, and in fact it hardly ever occurred. The first duty of man was to be constructive, to make things and make them well. Civil servants and the like were held in low esteem, because they were regarded as parasites, contributing nothing to the wealth of the Empire, and preferring security to the risks and rewards of private enterprise. No Beadle or Pears would ever admit to voting for anybody who wasn't a Tory; Socialism was an abomination, contrary to human nature, and sure to end in catastrophic ruin for everybody, while Liberalism wasn't much better. Money making and money spending were good, and money was meant to be enjoyed. Hospitality and charity were virtues of a high order, and participation in public work was a social duty, especially for members of the male sex.

I learned one of the most important lessons from the attitude of my ancestors to their employees, who, no matter whether they were dock hands, factory workers, farm labourers or domestic servants were treated as persons, not as a commodity called 'labour'. Sometimes they were treated toughly, but never impersonally. My Great Uncle Frank, who was my grandfather's partner in Beadle Brothers, when faced with the threat of a strike for more wages by the stevedores at the Erith wharf, invited them to choose their best fighter and form a ring. Uncle Frank would take on the champion in single combat, and the strike would be settled by the outcome of the fight. The men agreed, and, when Uncle Frank knocked the champion down, they went happily back to work without their rise. Though the condition of most wage earners in those days was bad by modern standards, there were many employers, and my family amongst them, who had a strong sense of obligation and often affection for their work people as individuals. Of course this was paternalism, which is unfashionable now; but a little more paternalism today would be no bad thing.

Immediately after my father's death in 1917 when I was just eighteen, my mother, without so far as I can remember consulting me, decided to get me into her family business, which by this time had become part of the great Lever combine. So she went to see Lord Leverhulme and extracted from him an encouraging answer to her request that he should take me into the business when I was ready. I was not really very interested; I was due to go into the army in a few weeks; most of my friends had been slaughtered on the battlefields of Flanders in an incredibly short time after joining the army, and I saw no reason to suppose it would not happen to me. So I had little concern with the future and was mainly occupied with having a good time in the present. Fifteen months later in the outskirts of Mons, I received the ceasefire and suddenly became a man with a future, which was a sobering experience.

After taking my degree at Cambridge in 1921, I joined Lever Brothers at Port Sunlight in Cheshire, working in the soap factory and living in rather dingy lodgings in Rockferry. I found some interest in the work, and I liked the rather unenthusiastic people I worked with, but I disliked the life. I was far away from my family and friends and having too little money to go South for weekends, I was lonely. Nobody with authority in the business took any notice of me or seemed to be aware of my existence. I was subjected to a barrage of company propaganda but no personal attention, and I felt like a very small cog in a vast impersonal machine. This was not the sort of private enterprise which in my youth I had been taught to admire, and after more than a year of it, I decided to quit as soon as I could find another job. But there was very serious unemployment at the time, and it was extremely difficult to get a job of any kind. One day, to my surprise, I was sent for by the Managing Director, who praised my work and told me the company was about to make me assistant manager of one of their smaller factories. He began to speak encouragingly about my future prospects in Lever Brothers, which put me on the spot. Was I to let him go on in this vein or was I to come clean and confess that I was spiritually out of Lever Brothers already? I acted on impulse and came clean; I am sure he thought I was crazy, I half thought so myself; but he was very kind and wished me success. A month later I left and went south.

At about this time I renewed contact with a young woman I had known and admired at Cambridge, when she was at

Girton and I at Pembroke. Her name was Isobel Shields. She told me that she was the private secretary of a very remarkable man named John Reith, who was General Manager of something quite new called the British Broadcasting Company, which of course I had never heard of. She was convinced that it would grow into one of the most important and formidable influences in the country, and I listened to her, fascinated by her enthusiasm and by her faith in the value of the work she was doing, but it did not immediately occur to me that I too might play a part in it. Hers was the world of communication; mine the world of industry and commerce; hers was a strange world in which I did not know my way. But later she persuaded me to enter it, and I have never regretted it; she did me one of the best turns of my life.

This is why I went into the BBC, by accident and without any particular qualifications. I became a communicator at the age of twenty-four, having spent the whole of my previous life in an environment which had nothing to do with communications, unless commercial advertising can be included in that category. Many years later I met a director of Unilever, as it had then become, at a dinner party in London, and I told him the story of my defection from soap to broadcasting. He said that, had I remained, I should have been earning four times the money and my work would have been a quarter as interesting. I have no reason to suppose he was wrong.

CHAPTER 2

Life in the BBC

JOINING the BBC in September, 1923, was so different from joining it today that I had better give the reader some idea of what it was like. Few people had even heard of broadcasting and most of those who had regarded it as a stunt (they would have called it a gimmick today). It had no status, no established place in British life, and only a few people, with more than ordinary imagination, expected it to grow into anything except an amusing scientific toy, which half a million families might adopt at a price of ten shillings a year. After the first war various manufacturers of electrical apparatus had shown a desire to start broadcasting services in order to create a demand for radio receiving sets, and some had actually done so on a temporary experimental basis; but at the instigation of the Postmaster General they had been persuaded to pool their broadcasting ambitions and form a single company, in which every bona fide radio manufacturer could have a stake; and so in 1922 they registered the British Broadcasting Company Ltd. The directors, apart from the Chairman, were nominees of the principal manufacturers who had the largest holding of shares; six of them had invested £10,000 each, and the total investment was £71,000 on which it was hoped to pay a dividend of not more than $7\frac{1}{2}\%$. The company had been licensed by the Postmaster General to build up and conduct a national service of broadcasting for the United Kingdom. It started in November 1922 from an office in Magnet House, Kingsway, and a small studio in Marconi House, Strand. Reith, who arrived at the office on December 30th, describes it in his book *Into the Wind*, as a room about thirty feet by fifteen, furnished with three long tables and some chairs, and a tiny compartment about six feet square at the far end, which was to be the private office of the six foot seven General Manager. On the outer door there was a small painted board saying "BBC. Walk in", and that notice now adorns the board-room in Broadcasting House, serving as a perpetual reminder to later generations of the humble origins of British broadcasting.

This 'sardine tin' existence could not go on for long, and more spacious premises were soon found at No. 2 Savoy Hill, Strand, the home of the Institute of Electrical Engineers, which the BBC equipped with a studio and control room and a number of offices including a very large one for the giant General Manager. It was shortly after the move to Savoy Hill that I was conducted by Isobel Shields into the presence of the newly-appointed Assistant General Manager, Vice-Admiral Charles Carpendale, C.B., to offer my services. She had warned me to call him 'Sir' frequently and to give my age as twenty-five, because he did not like engaging young men under that age; he thought they were too immature for the BBC. As I was only twenty-four this was a bit awkward, but somehow I got round the difficulty, whether by vagueness or false pretences I do not remember, but it worked —I was in, and my life's career in broadcasting had begun.

What a man does is sometimes less important than the people he does it with, and I think this was so in my case during that first year in the BBC. The men I worked with were the founders of British broadcasting and it is to them that we owe the shape of things today. I will write briefly of a few of them in their chronological order, which is not necessarily the order of the value of their contributions, but it is the order of their appearance on the scene.

In the beginning the BBC was a group of engineers, drawn mainly from the Marconi Company, whose role was to develop the technique, without which no effective broadcasting was possible. Because the technique was very rudimentary in 1923, the BBC engineers were exceptionally important people, and it is an interesting fact that much of the prestige which they enjoyed then still attaches to them forty years later. (In this respect the BBC is quite different from newer broadcasting organizations, which engage engineers to drive efficient machinery designed and manufactured by others.) When I first joined, Captain P. P. Eckersley was the Chief Engineer. He was an exceptional engineer in that he saw beyond the technique, which was his speciality, and had a strong interest in the uses of the medium. He became famous for his brilliant impromptu talks to listeners. Also, there were Noel Ashbridge, Harold Bishop, and Rowland Wynn, to name only a few of the engineering pioneers who played a large part in my later life.

The directors of the company foresaw that the BBC could not long remain a predominantly engineering affair, and before the end of 1922 they appointed Arthur Burrows and Cecil Lewis to be Director of Programmes and Assistant Director respectively. These two men were particularly important to me when I came on the scene nine months later, because they were my first bosses. Burrows had been the Marconi Company's publicity officer. In the pre-BBC days he had probably done more than any other man to propagate the notion of broadcasting, to think out the social and political consequences, and to formulate a technique of communication through the new medium. I remember him as a fussy, kindly, round man, with unbounded enthusiasm for broadcasting. He always seemed to me to care more for the technique of communication than for the material to be communicated. Acoustics, the balance of musical instruments, the placing of microphones and above all the clarity of voice and diction were of vast importance to him. He carried his ideas of clear diction so far that when he had to use the word 'accumulator' on the air, he separated the second and third letters, thus pronouncing it as two words 'ac' 'cumulator'. (We did not at first discover that clear speech has nothing to do with spelling.) Burrows played a big part in the birth of broadcasting, but he lacked some of the qualities needed in a Director of Programmes. His assistant, Cecil Lewis, had more of them, and he made some really important contributions to the developing art of programming, especially on the artistic side. I was Lewis's assistant and I worked in the same office with him. He was a tall, fair-haired, good-looking young man with a very beautiful Russian wife, whom he had met in the Far East when he was in the Royal Flying Corps during the war. He was a colourful personality who lived in a perpetual state of rush, and in spite of the fact that he did most of the talking, (or perhaps because of it) we got on well together.

In December, 1922, the Directors appointed a General Manager. They chose John Reith, aged thirty-four, the son of a

Scottish minister, who after an English public school education had been apprenticed to a Glasgow engineering firm before the war. A distinguished war career had left him with a scar on the face, which has been one of his many assets ever since. This appointment was the most important thing that has ever happened in British broadcasting. Reith had been trained for an industrial career, but his early years in the manse and some post war political experience made him at home in the world of the communicators; and though broadcasting was quite new to him, he came to it with a ready-made understanding of its purposes. Some people seem to think Reith moulded British broadcasting to a pattern of his own design and made it a reflection of himself, but this I think is an overstatement. In spite of his compelling aspect he did not drive the BBC into his own personal pattern; rather he led it along paths which the staff, and many others outside the BBC, wished it to follow. The difference between Reith and most others lay in his clarity of mind, singleness of purpose and immense energy. These are the qualities of leadership and he exercised them to the full. Only in two respects did he attempt to take us beyond the current standards of our generation; these were manifested in his attitude to divorce and to the Sabbath. He got an exaggerated reputation for austerity; but he was a smoker and, though he did not drink alcohol himself, he was an extremely generous host. I have drunk more at Reith's table than I really wanted, because of his fear lest, through lack of experience, he should underestimate my capacity.

This was the young man who was presiding over the BBC with such consummate skill when I arrived in September, 1923. Our respect and admiration was in no way diminished by our fear of him (he was a rather frightening man and I think he knew it); but I have never known a less impersonal or more kindly man than Reith. He was intensely interested in persons and responded at once to approaches to himself as a person. I have never known a chief who cared so much about people, and this created an atmosphere which was a mixture of a happy family and a medieval court. Anything less like Port Sunlight would be hard to imagine.

Another character who played a large part in my early BBC life was 'The Admiral'—Vice-Admiral Charles Carpendale, C.B.

who was Reith's number two and deputy. He was a tall blue-eyed sailor with an infectious laugh and a tremendous sense of fun, which he could turn off at a moment's notice and assume an aspect of extreme severity. In 1923 he was a more mature man than Reith and less angular in some ways. In spite of a tendency to bluster when things were not entirely to his liking, he was immensely popular and one of the best loved men who have ever served the BBC. One of our number practised the art of imitating the Admiral, and would call his colleagues on the internal telephone and give them hell for some real or imaginary misdemeanour. This prank proved too dangerous and had to be abandoned.

My own work during the first year was very varied. We were just beginning what is now called networking, and it was my job to organize the network operations and make them fit with the local operations of each of the eight main stations. I was also responsible for the programme pages of the *Radio Times*, and this took me down to Fleet Street one night a week to help put the paper to bed. One or two nights a week and every other week-end I was the London announcer, and the first number of *Radio Times* bears my name as the announcer. This was before the days of John Snagge, Freddy Grisewood, Stewart Hibberd and others who became famous later. In my day the time signal was given by the announcer hitting the tubular bells an appropriate number of times, and on one occasion, when I had a cold, I was seized with an uncontrollable tickle in the throat which made me lose my nerve, and I marked nine o'clock with eleven strokes; I had lost count. Between noon and one o'clock we used to broadcast a very cheap programme intended to give the radio shops something to demonstrate their sets on. One announcer was training an entirely new boy in the announcing art, and he explained to the new boy that it was important to have one really long pianola record in the repertoire so that the announcer could go out and have his pint of beer at the Coal Hole in the Strand while the record was being played. They selected one which played for twenty-five minutes, got it started, went out and had their pint in a leisurely way, and returned to find the record still playing. The announcer enquired from the engineer in the control room whether everything was all right, and was told that it was, but the engineer thought the tune was a bit monotonous. They then discovered that the pianola had a fault; it was playing the same few bars over and over again and would have gone on doing so ad infinitum. The odd thing was that not a single listener complained to the BBC and so the miscreants got away with it.

I worked at Savoy Hill throughout my first year, which was one of the most rewarding of my life, because it was the year in which I found my feet and discovered a sphere of activity which I knew I could make my own—probably for life. I worked harder and for longer hours than I had previously thought possible, I learned a lot, and above all I was a member of a well-led team breaking new ground and believing in the value of what it was doing.

But this phase did not last long. A year after joining the BBC I began something which, with variations, was to be the main theme of my broadcasting career, an independent operational command. I accepted, at Reith's request, the job of head of the non-existent Durban Municipal Broadcasting Station in South Africa, and in December, 1924, three months after my arrival there, we were on the air. I was the head of a municipal department and my employers were the Borough Council, who, as might be expected, had none of the admirable self-restraint of the Parliament at Westminster. They knew better than I did how to run a broadcasting service, and once, when they were complaining about the announcing, the chairman of my committee, a publican of Scottish origin, said he could do it better himself. So confident was he that he readily accepted my invitation to take on the job for an evening. I sat with him in the studio, while he announced, but, having no telephonist, I was constantly being called away to the telephone, which worried him. At the end of the session, when he complained of my frequent absences, I had to confess, under pressure, that every call was a complaint about his announcing, in some cases accompanied by threats of withholding support for him at the next municipal elections. The advertisers were particularly censorious and after that I had no more trouble with the Council over announcing, and not much over anything else.

Though I had a lot of help from the Borough Electricity Department and its chief engineer, John Roberts, and a very useful source of orchestral programmes in the Durban Municipal

LIFE IN THE BBC

Orchestra under H. Lyall Taylor, my two years in Durban was an experience of broadcasting in the raw. Apart from these technical and orchestral facilities, no provision of any kind had been made for the conduct of a broadcasting service, and I was expected to be on the air for five or six hours a day six days a week without staff and with a programme allowance of almost negligible proportions. By constant battling I managed to get some staff, but it was inadequate in quantity and underpaid, with the result that I had to turn my hand to almost anything that needed doing. We formally opened the station on a sweltering hot night in the middle of a subtropical summer, and it was my job to accompany the Mayor and receive His Excellency the Governor of Natal on the steps of the Town Hall, in which building our studio was situated. Of course I was dressed in the conventional boiled shirt and white tie, but for an hour before the Governor's arrival I was on my hands and knees with dustpan and brush sweeping up the mess in the studio, which an idle Zulu house boy had failed to do before going off duty. I had to beg people to broadcast, preferably without fee, but I generally had to give them half a guinea for two groups of songs or a fifteen minute talk. Sometimes I even went as high as a guinea for exceptional talent, but this was rare. We ignored the existence of copyright, though towards the end of my two years we had a visit from a representative of the Performing Rights Society and had to come to some sort of terms with him.

I had never written a play and never, since early childhood, acted in one, but I had to do both in Durban, and I was a daily performer in the Children's Hour under the pseudonym of 'Uncle Tim', reading stories and indulging in various forms of juvenile backchat. We started a weekly publication which was called *Durban Calling* to publicize our programmes because the newspapers wouldn't print them; and because there was nobody else to do it I had to be its editor, writing an article for each issue, arranging the format and correcting proofs.

Most of the programmes came from our single studio in the Town Hall building, which had no forced ventilation, let alone air conditioning, and the Durban climate in summer is very hot and humid, rather like Singapore they tell me. The studio was often like the Black Hole of Calcutta, but it fortunately had windows, which for acoustic reasons were supposed to be kept shut. For the sake of survival we had to throw them open on many occasions and put up with the traffic noises which became superimposed on the programmes. Nobody seemed to mind very much, and the up-country people positively enjoyed the clanging of the trams and the calls of the rickshaw boys, because it brought a taste of the city into their isolated lives. After a time we even used the traffic noises as an interval signal, or a space to fill up time when we were short of advertisements.

We earned our living in two ways—a licence fee of thirty-five shillings a year and advertising, which was mainly publicising the Durban shops and the goods they had in stock at the moment. The advertisements, which I often had to read myself, were unpopular with the public, so towards the end of my time we abandoned them in response to public opinion, and because the expansion of the licence revenue made advertising money progressively less important to us. The Durban Municipal Broadcasting Station was a pretty parochial affair with little hope of ever becoming anything more, and after about eighteen months I submitted a memorandum to the Town Council recommending a merger with the broadcasting stations in Cape Town and Johannesburg with the ultimate objective of a national system for the whole of the Union of South Africa. In spite of the fact that this would have meant the withdrawal of the Durban Corporation from the broadcasting business, it had a good reception there and a very favourable press throughout the Union, but it did not come about in my time. Shortly after my return home it did happen, when all the stations were acquired by the entertainment monopoly of the Schlezinger interests. Later it was nationalized on a plan recommended by Reith and called the South African Broadcasting Corporation. I received a cable a few years later when I was in Belfast, asking me whether I was prepared to go back to South Africa as Director General of the national system, and not being very keen to leave Britain again just then I quoted a price for my services which was more than they were prepared to pay.

Towards the end of my contract period I received an offer from Reith to return as the British Broadcasting Company's Director in Northern Ireland, which I accepted without hesitation. It was another independent operational command, and I took up my duties in Belfast in October, 1926, staying there for

LIFE IN THE BBC

the next six years. It was during this period that the Company was nationalized by a Tory Government under Mr. Baldwin, and renamed the British Broadcasting Corporation; Reith was knighted; Broadcasting House was built in Portland Place out of the profits on the *Radio Times*; the BBC was growing up.

It was a great relief to be working again for a specialized broadcasting company, and not for a municipal corporation with no understanding of the broadcasting business. The BBC's Northern Ireland operation had been going on for two years, so mine was not exactly a pioneering job; rather it was a task of consolidation, which meant building the BBC into the lives of the people of the province and making it one of their public institutions. When I arrived in Northern Ireland I was made to feel for the first time in my life that I was a person of some public importance, and this was in spite of the fact that the BBC was less than four years old and its Northern Ireland operation not much more than two. Obviously the BBC's prestige had grown out of all recognition during my two years' absence in South Africa, and I, as its chief local representative, shared the fruits of it. I was invited to become a member of the Ulster Club, where almost daily I met members of the Government; the Governor, the Duke of Abercorn, was immensely helpful and friendly, and Lord Craigavon, the Prime Minister, was a keen supporter of our work. In effect I was made a member of the Establishment of a province which had most of the paraphernalia of a sovereign state and a population no bigger than a moderate sized English county.

My six years there turned out to be a period of difficult relations between the BBC's regions and the Headquarters at Savoy Hill, because the new Director of Programmes in London, Roger Eckersley, elder brother of P. P. Eckersley, had realized that the newly-perfected network made it possible to concentrate programme production on London and feed the rest of the country from there. This in turn would enable the BBC to concentrate more money and talent at the centre and thus raise programme standards for the whole country. The regional controllers opposed this form of centralization as damaging to the proper reflection of local life and talent, which was their special concern. There was good sense and logic on both sides of the argument, and a reasonable compromise was needed; but it was not reached during that six years; indeed so far as sound radio was concerned I do not think it was fully reached till after the war when Sir William Haley regionalized the Home Service. (The same clash existed in television during the whole of my term as Director, but in that medium no compromise satisfactory to both interests can be achieved till the BBC gets its second TV programme.) It was largely due to the inevitable clash of interests that regional controllers were encouraged to spend a lot of their time in London. I calculate that I crossed the Irish Sea, generally by night, about a hundred and fifty times in the six years between 1926 and 1932—and that was long before the journey could be done by air. In a further attempt to maintain regional harmony Reith appointed a travelling liaison officer, a job which was held successively by Douglas Clarke, Lindsay Wellington, Charles Siepman and in the end by Roger Eckersley himself.

Northern Ireland had one important characteristic in common with South Africa, in that both were peoples divided against themselves; an unhappy state of affairs in both countries and one which a broadcaster could not escape. It taught me that the fundamental unity of the English is a great blessing and something they do not always appreciate as much as they should.

In South Africa I had been much impressed with the strength of the demand amongst English-speaking people for a broadcasting service direct from 'home'—as they called it. This, of course, was not possible until we could devise a method of transmitting programmes over seven thousand miles or more, but by 1932 the BBC had done it, and was about to start an Empire Broadcasting Service. I applied for the job of Director, and it was a close thing between me and Cecil Graves (later Sir Cecil Graves), who was finally chosen, while I was offered and accepted the job he vacated, Assistant Director of Programmes in London, under Roger Eckersley who was Director. I did this job for four years, and it turned out to be an important part of my training. I was still rather young, and for eight of my nine years of broadcasting service I had been in independent commands; so I was probably getting too independent for a young man of thirty-three. During this period I came in for a good deal of moulding by Reith, probably unconscious on his part, and it did me a lot of good. At one point he nominated me as the first Director General of All India Radio, because he had been asked by the Viceroy to nominate someone. It was another independent operational command and therefore attractive to me, but the salary of £1,800 was absurdly low, quite inadequate for a young man with a wife and family to educate in England and without private means. I asked for £3,000 and after a lot of haggling with the Indian High Commissioner I discovered they were paying their Director of Civil Aviation, which seemed to me a relatively minor job in those days, a good deal more than they were offering me; so I withdrew and my Indian career was thus nipped in the bud.

An interesting sideline at this time was my chairmanship of the Concerts Committee, a body which managed all the BBC's public concerts, the Proms, the winter symphony concerts in the Queen's Hall, the provincial and foreign tours of the BBC Symphony Orchestra, and any other public concerts involving paying audiences. It was a business job and not an artistic one. For a time I was also chairman of the London Concerts Committee, on which the major promoters of orchestral concerts in London were represented, and whose function was to coordinate all concerts in the capital so as to avoid clashing interests. I enjoyed this work, because though not a musician I am devoted to music, and I came to know well a number of distinguished musicians, including Sir Henry Wood, Sir Adrian Boult, Sir Hamilton Harty and others. It once fell to my lot to give dinner to Toscanini and his wife, an experience which would have been more inspiring if we had understood each other's languages a little better.

For six months during this period I had yet another side line, which arose from the fact that J. C. Stobart became very ill and was in fact a dying man. His job was Director of Religious Broadcasting, and I was instructed by Reith to take over Stobart's duties in addition to my other numerous functions, which I did, though I had only the slenderest qualifications for the task. It is the one occasion in my life when I have been the head of a specialized programme producing department. I became involved in negotiations for the celebration of the centenary of the Anglo-Catholic movement in the Church of England and found myself in a veritable hornet's nest of strong feelings, of which I had previously been but vaguely aware; and the fact that Stobart himself shared those feelings did not make my task any easier. My only public performances in connection with the job were occasional readings of the Epilogue on Sunday evenings, and this was a very tricky thing to do, because Reith took a strong personal interest in the Epilogue and never missed hearing it. After Stobart's death the Reverend Frederick Iremonger was appointed to take his place, and with much relief I handed over the job to this fine man, who as 'Freddy" soon became one of the most popular members of the BBC staff. He left us at the beginning of the war to become Dean of Litchfield.

By the early nineteen thirties programme production for broadcasting had passed beyond the amateur stage of trial and error, and in the hands of a lot of talented young men and women it was developing into a highly skilled profession. It was, of course, an amalgam of the technical and the artistic, which required good team work between technicians and producers, but the higher command of the BBC were strangely slow to recognize the emergence of the professionalism which after all was the very basis of their business. Morale amongst the operational staff suffered, because individuals tried to make lines of demarkation for themselves and the rivalries of different schools of thought were becoming troublesome. The feeling between engineers and producers was particularly acute.

It seemed to me that the BBC needed a repository of professional knowledge and experience, and some method by which producers and studio engineers could have access to it; also it needed a focal point for its professionalism. I said all this to Reith, and some time later he sent for me and told me that the Governors had accepted my view, and proposed to set up a staff training school, which I was to start and devote my whole time to. Thus for the first and only time in my life I became the headmaster of a sort of academic institution. I was given carte blanche to engage thirty of the best young men and women I could find and to train them as broadcasters. I was given a very experienced programme man, Archie Harding, as chief instructor, and between us we chose our first batch of students, most of whom have done very well since, some occupying high positions in the BBC today, and some in commercial television too. A few, including Guy Burgess, are no longer with us. The BBC Training School became for broadcasting what the Staff College is for the soldiers, a focal point of professionalism, and soon there was a big demand from abroad. We found ourselves training broadcasters from most of the countries in the Commonwealth and from many foreign countries too. Though I was headmaster for only a year, I was a regular lecturer at the school for the next twenty-five years.

The lure of the independent operational command caught up with me again in 1937. The BBC had not previously had a West of England Region because of a shortage of channels, but now the difficulty had been overcome and the new region was to be inaugurated. Applications for the job of Regional Controller were numerous, and in spite of Reith's dissuasion, I could not resist the temptation to enter myself. There was a large appointments board, the only one I have ever attended in my life as a candidate, and I got the job, which I did not finally vacate until 1956, nineteen years later, when I became Director of Television in London.

One day in the summer of 1938, on a visit to London from the West, I put my head round Reith's door and asked him to lunch with me at my club. He readily accepted saying that it would suit him very well because the club was on the way to Downing Street, where he had an appointment in the early afternoon. In the taxi he told me he was leaving the BBC to become head of Imperial Airways, and that was what he was going to see the Prime Minister about. That same evening his transfer was publicly announced and it caused much more sorrow than surprise in the BBC. Reith for a long time had been bored, because he did not feel himself to be 'fully stretched' (an expression he used about himself in 'Face to Face' on BBC Television more than twenty years later). For example, he had told the War Minister that his time was almost all spare; he could do his BBC work in an hour a day and devote the rest of the day and most of the night, if need be, to another occupation. After fifteen years of immense labour he had succeeded in creating a unique national institution, and, for the time being at any rate, his creative act was over; he needed fresh fields to conquer. Many years later he chided me for not having insisted over the lunch table on his staying with the BBC; but who was I to throw my weight about in a matter of such high politics?

So Reith left and was succeeded by Frederick Ogilvie, Vice-Chancellor of Queen's University, Belfast. A year later the war broke out and prearranged plans for evacuating the BBC's non-political activities from London were put into immediate operation. Most of the larger producing departments descended on my regional headquarters in Bristol, and studios had to be improvised in church halls and in any building we could find which offered sufficient space. Several hundreds of BBC staff and artists were billeted in the homes of Bristol's hospitable citizens, and it was from that city that most of the programmes came during the early years of the war. I was in charge of this extraordinary exercise in improvisation, and I remember on one occasion buying a house, which I had no authority to do. This led to a protracted and acrimonious correspondence with headquarters, which was not settled till a year later when I became the Director of Administration in London; one of my first acts on taking over my new duties was to send for the correspondence, authorize the purchase of the house and add a minute to the effect that the West Regional Controller had shown commendable enterprise in buying it.

In addition to my other responsibilities I became a Company Commander in the Home Guard, my first duty being to form a BBC Company of four platoons. The BBC Symphony Orchestra made up one platoon under its commander Sir Adrian Boult, and a very fine platoon it was with Paul Beard as sergeant and Eugene Cruft as corporal. One day there was a routine rifle inspection in the guard-room and a well-known actor, who shall remain anonymous, had forgotten to unload. The bullet went through the ceiling and narrowly missed Derek McCulloch, who was sitting in his office above. As we were under military discipline this incident had to come before the Battalion Commander and the actor was sentenced to a period of detention as laid down in King's Regulations. As he was playing the lead in a play that very night, I had to plead for a mitigation of sentence, which was readily granted and we never heard any more about it.

There was an important interlude for me during the war. No matter what the members of BBC staff did during the war, they had to do it in a temporary acting capacity; our pre-war jobs remained our substantive appointments, and we were expected to go anywhere and do anything required of us as long as the war lasted. In the autumn of 1940, the early stage of the blitz, I was ordered to London by Ogilvie, the Director General, to be the Director of Administration. This meant my working immediately under Ogilvie and becoming a member of the Board of Management. It proved to be one of the most extraordinary experiences of my official life. The Board of Governors had been reduced to two, a Chairman and a Vice-Chairman, the internal management was chaotic, the licence revenue was being pocketed by the Government, and the BBC for the first and only time in its history was living on Government grants. The Ministry of Information was directing all programmes, which in its own opinion had any bearing on the war effort, and it was even concerning itself with internal staff appointments. For the first time I realized to the full what the BBC had lost in Reith's departure two years earlier. It would have been a difficult situation even for Reith to cope with, but he would have done it as he did with the General Strike in 1926. In the special circumstances of the war some compromise with the BBC's traditional independence from government was inevitable if the BBC was to play its full part, and a radical adaptation of the administrative machine was essential to keep pace with the tremendous demands being made upon it; but all this called for bold and experienced leadership, which unhappily was lacking. The BBC had been made responsible for the projection of Britain to the world through radio and so it had become an important instrument of war. The staff increased from four thousand to about fourteen thousand within three years; accommodation had to be found; premises were often destroyed overnight by bombs and more had to be found; there were big problems of evacuation, which gave rise to many human difficulties, and above all the highly centralized pre-war administrative machine, built up by Reith in peace time, proved far too slow for the fast-moving wartime situation. I sought leave to change it by delegating day-to-day administration to the operational divisions and departments, but it was not until 1942 when Robert Foot, an experienced industrial administrator, succeeded Ogilvie, who left and later became Principal of Jesus College Oxford, that I found support for my thinking. Foot and I carried it out almost immediately. The job of Director of Administration was abolished and I was made Principal Assistant to the Joint Directors-General. (The other Director General being Sir Cecil Graves—a very wise but sick man, who shortly had to retire through ill health.)

Then a very odd situation arose. I expected to control what was left of the central administration on behalf of the Director General, but he decided to do most of it himself, and so I was left with the softest job I have ever had in my life. By Foot's time the BBC had been got into top gear as a war machine, there was a long lull in the bombing of London, the important policy side of programming was directed by government departments, and the artistic and entertainment side was in the experienced hands of Mr (later Sir) Basil Nicolls. There was less policy than usual for the Director General to direct, but there was the internal administration, and the financial control.

At this time I did a very foolish thing. At my home in Gloucestershire one week-end I humped fifty hundredweight sacks of agricultural lime and cracked a spinal disc, which gave me intense pain from which I could get no relief, and in 1943 I resumed my substantive job of West Regional Controller. This meant I could live at home in Gloucestershire under my wife's care and get some treatment for my injury, but in fact I remained partially disabled, and often in pain, until eight years later, when an accurate diagnosis followed by an operation in 1951 put me completely right.

There was an unbroken spell as West Regional Controller lasting from 1943 to 1956, the longest uninterrupted period of office I ever had, and one of the most rewarding. As soon as the war in Europe was over I got into touch with Frank Gillard, a proper Westcountryman, who before the war had been a schoolmaster in Taunton and during the war a BBC war correspondent. He accepted my invitation to become head of the programme side, the most important office in any region short of Controller, and together we succeeded in building up a first-rate staff of programme producers, whose talents reflected the life and interests of the West Country to an extent never previously achieved. The BBC under Sir William Haley had regained its full peacetime independence, and Haley had regionalized the Home Service, thus making it possible for the first time in BBC history for local affairs to be properly represented in broadcasting. We had a clear field in front of us, and took every possible advantage of it both in programmes of regional interest and in contributions to the national networks. In the latter category 'Any Questions?' and the natural history programmes are especially worth mentioning. I remember one occasion when we were accidentally guilty of a breach of Parliamentary privilege in 'Any Questions?' A special White Paper was placed before Parliament and I was summoned to London to answer for the crime. In the course of discussion with Haley, he asked me whether, if an individual had to bear the blame and be incarcerated in the Tower of London, it should be the producer, or, if not him, who should it be? I said I thought the Director General was the most suitable scapegoat, but he said he was too busy and would nominate the Regional Controller, whereupon I told him I was expecting something like that and had brought a few extra shirts and underclothes with me. In the end we were let off with a caution.

Having had quite a lot of pre-war experience of presiding over special committees of investigation into this that or the other, I was asked in 1952 by Haley to be chairman of a BBC Economy Committee, sitting in London. Our job, lasting about three months, was to investigate every aspect of BBC expenditure not directly bearing on programme standards, and to recommend ways in which money could be saved without damage to the interests of the viewers and listeners. We were agreeably impressed at finding how few pockets of wastefulness there were, but we found certain areas in which we thought savings could be made. Some of our recommendations were acted upon immediately, while others, though shelved at the time, were put into effect later. It was an interesting committee drawn from very diverse spheres of BBC activity, one member being Hugh Carleton Greene of the External Services, whom I had not met before, and who together with his American wife Elaine became a close friend thereafter. (Now that he has become Director General he looks back on the 1952 Economy Committee as an important introduction to a side of life which is vital to him in his present high office.) The setting up of this committee was characteristic of Haley, whose régime was marked by a most strict regard for economy and good financial management; but lest it should be thought that he lacked expansiveness I must record that it was Haley who conceived the BBC Television Centre and bought the White City site on which it now stands. This is one of the most expansive things the BBC has ever done, and Haley would have built it much earlier, if the Government had not put the brake on BBC capital expenditure for ten years after the end of the war.

The thirteen post-war years as West Regional Controller were very valuable to me in a personal way too, because they allowed me to put down roots, something I had always wanted to do, but never had the chance to do before. For the first time in my life I bought a house with the intention of making it a permanent home, and that house is still my home and probably will remain so to the end. I was able to play some part in local affairs, for instance by representing my own and a neighbouring parish on the Rural District Council, for which, by the way, I had to fight an election as an Independent; both Tories and Socialists voted for me, thinking in each case that I was one of them; I don't know why. I became Chairman of my Parish Council, Church Warden and Treasurer, Correspondent of the village school, a Governor of the Wiltshire County College and of Badminton School for girls in Bristol. I was a member of the Bristol Diocesan Board of Finance and of the Council of the Bath and West Society. When I was transferred to London in 1956 I had to give up nearly all these local activities, because I became little more than a week-end visitor to the West and my whole attention was directed elsewhere.

By the time I was fully restored to health which was about 1953 every BBC directorship in London, except Administration, which I did not want, was filled by a younger man than me, and I had the prospect—the very agreeable prospect—of remaining West Regional Controller until my retirement. But in 1956 something quite unexpected happened. Sir George Barnes, the Director of Television, four years younger than me, accepted the Vice-Chancellorship of a university, and at the age of fifty-seven I was appointed Director of Television, holding the job for five years until my retirement in 1961. It was the directorship which I wanted above all others. In the early stages of life luck is comparatively unimportant, because time is on one's side; but in the final stages of a career luck is everything, and I was lucky.

I was not entirely new to television, because the opening of the Wenvoe transmitter in 1952 had brought it to the West Country, and so for the ensuing four years I had been in charge of a developing television operation, albeit on a relatively small scale. Though I was fifth in the line of succession, I was in fact the first Director of Television to come to the job with a background of experience in the new medium, though I must admit that experience of the particular medium is less important to a director than general experience of broadcasting, and that I had in large measure. There was not very much about the job that was new to me in kind, but in scale it was the biggest operational command I had ever had, and it was certainly one of the most stimulating. I owed a great deal to my predecessors, Cock, Gorham, Collins and Barnes, who, in spite of many difficulties and frustrations had left me with a service of which I could be immensely proud. My staff were the most important factor of all, and I shall never cease to be grateful for their professional skill and their talents in a very wide variety of specialized fields. In particular I was splendidly served by the four Controllers who worked immediately under me, Kenneth Adam (programmes), Stuart Williams (administration), Seymour de Lotbiniere (programme services) and Martin Pulling (engineering). I think few chiefs are better served by their senior officers than I was during that five years. There was one other, Ronald Waldman, whom I appointed at a later stage to manage our rapidly increasing overseas commercial activities—the buying, and more importantly the selling of programmes, and all the exceedingly complex negotiations which go with them, together with the making of television programmes by the British film industry with the financial backing of the BBC. Waldman as a General Manager worked immediately under me, and together we found ourselves operating in a world of international big business which was new to the BBC.

The BBC is probably the most comprehensive broadcasting corporation in the world in that it controls three very diverse groups of services, Home Sound Radio, Television and External Sound Radio, each having a service director. Presiding over the directors is a Director General, who is the immediate servant of the Board of Governors, and so it comes about that the Director General is of very great importance to every director. During most of my term as Director of Television my Director General was Sir Ian Jacob, who had been promoted from the External Services when Sir William Haley left to become Editor of *The Times* in 1952. One of his many assets was his quite remarkable physical health and stamina, which during his term of office never seemed to let him down in spite of the fact that he did not spare himself day or night. Fortunately for me his attitude towards television was one of rapid expansion, and if there had ever been reason to suspect the BBC of going slow with television, Jacob dispelled it. His energy was such that he would have liked personally to have controlled News, Current Affairs, Religious and Educational Broadcasting for the whole BBC; indeed he went a long way towards doing so, which added sometimes to the complexity of my job. However, his interest in these and other programme matters was entirely constructive, and in the sphere of sport for television he was especially energetic. I was the first BBC service director to be placed in a competitive position and I was helped enormously by Jacob's expansive support and his generous allocation of funds in spite of our perpetual uncertainty about the BBC's financial future.

It had been a matter of puzzlement to me how Parliament had been induced to swallow the Television Act of 1954, but I soon discovered a quite remarkable lack of information about broadcasting and especially about the BBC on the part of most Members of Parliament. I had no doubt this was our fault; the range of subject matter which comes before members is so vast that it is quite impossible for them to have a real grasp of more than a small fraction of it. Broadcasting, which in a special sense is neither free nor private, depends absolutely on their decisions, and it seemed important for me to keep members in touch with BBC Television as far as that was possible. And so I usually made a point of being present at the studios to entertain any Members of Parliament and Ministers who were taking part in programmes, and in addition we used to invite groups of members to visit us for demonstrations and expositions of our work. From 1960 onwards we were tremendously helped by the completion of the new Television Centre at Shepherd's Bush, because it signifies in a very spectacular way the primacy of the

LIFE IN THE BBC

BBC Television Service both at home and in the world at large. Our visitors were thus more readily able to appreciate the value of the great national asset for which in the last resort they are responsible. Now under the new Director General, Hugh Carleton Greene, the explanatory process is being carried still further, and no opportunities are being missed to assist Members of Parliament and others in authority to an understanding of the very complex pattern of British broadcasting. But all this, in addition to one's normal work, means long hours and late nights, and my usual working day was from 9.30 a.m. to midnight with an occasional siesta between 6.0 and 7.0 p.m.

Another of my many extra duties was to act as host on all appropriate occasions, and the number of such occasions was considerable. Most of the members of our own Royal Family, and some foreign ones too, visited us during my time, and we had Prime Ministers from most of the Commonwealth countries and a host of other well-known and distinguished people from various parts of the world. I shall never forget the astonished and delighted expression on the face of a young waitress when in the course of dinner with me the Aga Khan spoke of his enthusiasm for jazz; nor shall I forget Sir Anthony Eden, the Prime Minister, being mistaken for a lunatic, when a few minutes before a broadcast he slipped into an ill-lit empty room and started rehearsing out loud a few sentences of his speech. It was the commissionaire's locker room, and one of them, who had had the job of ejecting a real lunatic earlier in the day, discovered Sir Anthony and immediately raised the alarm that another lunatic was at large on BBC premises. On one occasion I gave a late supper party for Vice-President and Mrs. Nixon, and after it was over I accompanied them and the American Ambassador and his wife to their car. After an exchange of courtesies I closed the door and the car was just about to move off, when Mrs. Nixon put her head out of the window and said, "Where is the Vice-President?" I said, "Haven't you got him in there?" She said "No." There was an immense crowd milling about in the street, and I told a burly commissionaire to make a way through to the centre of it. There I found the Vice-President of the United States signing autograph albums, and told him I thought it would be advisable for him to get back into the car. He took my advice, but I thought with a certain amount of reluctance.

My transfer from a Regional Controllership to the Directorship of Television meant a move from a domestic activity into one with world-wide ramifications, and this involved me in a certain amount of travel, but not as much as I should have liked. I paid short visits to the television authorities in France, Italy, Belgium and Canada, but I spent much more time in the United States of America, visiting it four or five times during my term of office. I have come to know the States so well (incidentally I spent another three months there after my retirement), and I have made so many good friends over there that I now almost regard it as my second home, especially is this so of New York, which I love. But my work has taken me to many other parts of the States, the West Coast, the Middle West, Washington and the South; indeed many of my American friends say I have seen more of their country than they have. It is a country for which in most respects I have enormous admiration, but I cannot include their television, a sphere in which I think they have gone right off the rails, and most thoughtful Americans think so too. Their political climate and their constitution make it very difficult for them to assimilate television as a comprehensive medium of communication, because this would require a degree of regulation by the central (or federal) Government, which in principal is anathema to every normal American except in the spheres of defence and foreign policy. And yet broadcasting by its very nature is unmanageable by any other means, and so the Americans are in a broadcasting dilemma. If in this book I appear to my American readers to dwell overmuch on the inadequacy of their television, I hope they will not think me guilty of discourtesy to a great and very friendly neighbour. My reason for stressing these things is that certain misguided persons in my own country, where the prevailing political philosophy makes the assimilation of broadcasting much easier, have been propagating the notion that we should follow the American pattern; and I think it is important that the British people should have some idea of what that pattern is and how relatively fortunate are we who live in a small, thickly-populated country with a centralized, democratic government, which by popular consent is permitted to regulate broadcasting in the public interest.

Since John Reith left the BBC in 1938 he has done many great things and received many honours including a barony; throughout all this time he has been most friendly and kind to me personally, but his relations with the BBC have often been regrettably cool; and so it was a great joy to me that during my last two years he was a visitor to Television Centre, lunching or dining with me there on a number of occasions. He and my wife and I lunched together at Claridges on my return from being knighted by the Queen Mother at Buckingham Palace, and on the evening before my last day in the BBC he dined with us at the Centre, presenting me with an inscribed copy of the *Oxford English Dictionary* to mark my retirement. I have always said that Reith is a very personal man.

CHAPTER 3

The Birth of Public Television

SOME time about 1933 or 1934, I was summoned by the Admiral (by then Sir Charles Carpendale) and instructed to prepare a financial estimate for a television service. This was my first television job. I knew it was no good asking him what kind of a service it was to be, because he didn't know any better than I did. Nobody knew. So I took my order, left the room and started to think; my thinking got me nowhere. I had a friend named Gerald Cock, who was head of the Outside Broadcasting department and more closely in touch with the outside world of public entertainment, sport and motion picture production, than I was at that time. He was a man of great imagination, unbounded enthusiasm and energy, also he was the nearest thing to a real professional broadcaster among my close friends. So I went to him and asked him to help me. Between us we made a lot of hypothetical assumptions, in which we ourselves had no great faith; but we needed a basis for calculation. In the end we came to the conclusion that a television service would probably cost not less than ten times as much as a sound service of comparable scope and quality, so, instead of presenting the Admiral with a complicated set of figures, I gave him four words, 'Sound multiplied by ten', and he accepted it. I have been agreeably astonished ever since to note how nearly accurate that original estimate was. Little did either Cock or I know at the time that he would be the first chief of the world's first television service and that I would inherit the position twenty years later.

And now in 1962 I have consulted Cock again. He directed the service during its three pre-war years, when it was the only public television service in the world. (I was serving in the West Region miles out of television range.) Cock writes:

THE BIRTH OF PUBLIC TELEVISION

'In 1935 the BBC accepted responsibility for establishing and running an 'Experimental service of television' using (subject to later revision) two radically different systems alternately. The Alexandra Palace was chosen as the site and a rental agreement with its trustees followed. Reconstruction of the old building was begun, under the able supervision of M. T. Tudsbery, the BBC's civil engineer. By the summer of 1936 studio equipment, transmitters and antennae had been installed, and the Post Office had laid a TV carrying cable round the West End for outside broadcasts. The staff then moved in and test programmes were put out as soon as they had acquired a working knowledge of the apparatus. In August, 1936, a number of somewhat primitive programmes were televised to and from Radio Olympia. Soon afterwards the programme hours were extended and a fairly regular service began. In the meantime BBC and EMI (Electrical and Musical Industries Ltd) engineers had managed to reduce breakdowns to negligible proportions when operating the electronic system and as far as possible when operating the Baird system, the installation of which was not completed until some weeks later. From the early days it was obvious to the staff that television had a brilliant future, but that the 'two system' working was going to keep it back and add greatly to our difficulties. In the autumn of 1936 a visit by the technical and international press was arranged; and on November 2nd the official opening took place. Then on February 2nd, following my report on the subject, single system working began and the real Television Service, as we know it today, followed.

'In May, 1937, the first portable outside broadcast equipment ever to be built was delivered direct to Hyde Park Corner by EMI in time for a very successful transmission of the coronation procession on May 6th, using the special cable connection with Alexandra Palace. Thereafter the TV service never looked back, and was soon extended to approximately six hours a day for seven days a week. With the arrival of a portable transmitter outside broadcast events up to twenty-five miles from Alexandra Palace were made available. Sales of receivers increased rapidly and this brought rather more generous financial support from Broadcasting House. The peak of the service was probably reached in the early summer of 1939. Thereafter key staff began to be called up for national service. On September 1, 1939, the service closed down without apology or explanation to its viewers. War had come to wipe the slate clean of three years intensive effort. When in 1944 the Hankey Committee was formed to recommend future policy, few people seemed to remember that there had been a regular TV service in this country only five years earlier.'

This is Gerald Cock's own account of those three unique years of television pioneering. By 1939 about 20,000 receiving sets were in use in the London area, and one manufacturer reported that his orders for television receivers exceeded those for sound by about three to two. If it had not been for the war Britain's lead in television would have been even greater than it is today.

Looking back on the programmes of BBC Television during those three years one cannot help being amazed at the range of the subject matter and the great distinction of so many of the artists and speakers. The coronation procession, the Derby, and cup finals all found their way into the programmes. Success on this scale could not have been achieved without a highly-skilled staff, well led and bubbling over with enthusiasm. Enormous credit is due to these devoted men and women, and it was a matter of great satisfaction to me that so many of them were still in the service with me when I was Director during the 1956-1961 period. In November, 1957, we celebrated the twenty-first birthday of the service by giving a dinner in the original studio in Alexandra Palace to as many of the pre-war pioneers as could be gathered together. It was a nostalgic and impressive occasion, but unfortunately Gerald Cock was in California and too far away to get to the dinner; however, there had been an exchange of telegrams between him and me. Leonard Schuster, who had been the chief administrative officer, and had since retired, spoke for the pioneers who were no longer with us. Douglas Birkinshaw and Cecil Madden spoke for those who were still in the service, while the Director General, Sir Ian Jacob and the Director of Engineering, Sir Harold Bishop, paid very warm tributes to the founder members, absent and present, of the world's first television service.

But there seems to have been a fly in the ointment. Both before, and for several years after, the war there was a strong feeling amongst successive heads of the television service, Gerald Cock, Maurice Gorham and Norman Collins, that television was not being taken seriously enough by the BBC, that it was being treated too much as the Cinderella and a mere appendage of sound radio. According to Cock, who has kindly provided me with some notes for this book, the 'Go slow' attitude was by no means peculiar to the BBC. I quote Cock:

'Unfortunately Reith was something less than enthusiastic about television. He has recently said that he was "always afraid of television". It is hard to believe that this Cromwellian character has ever been afraid of anything. I interpret his remark to mean that he had foreseen the present calamitous abuse of TV throughout the world. Reith incidentally was not alone in his dislike of TV. In 1944 Sir William Haley, then Editor-in-Chief and later Director General, saw his first demonstration of EMI television at Hayes. He commented to its then Managing Director in my presence that he wouldn't have a television set in his home. And at a luncheon given for me by William Paley, head of the Columbia Broadcasting System in New York in 1939, he, Paley, remarked rather glumly that, had it not been for our success at Alexandra Palace, the United States would not so soon have been faced with this threat to their network prosperity. Even as late as the post-war period the CBS radio network tried unsuccessfully to organize a campaign to postpone TV "pending improvements". David Sarnoff, too, head of the Radio Corporation of America and the National Broadcasting Company (whose Iconoscope had been developed by Vladimir Zworykin in the RCA Camden, New Jersey, research station, parallel with the British Emitron at EMI at Hayes under the brilliant leadership of Isaac Schoenberg, the late Alan Blumlein and Cecil Brown) was cagey about television as late as 1940 when I had a talk to him on the subject in New York. Sarnoff said television would have to "make its own future", whatever that meant. Clearly he too was not going to force the pace at the expense of his sound radio interests. Here in England the Radio Manufacturers' Association, with notable exceptions, were unenthusiastic.' (Cock mentions C. O. Stanley as one of the exceptions.)

TELEVISION: A CRITICAL REVIEW

Here we have a situation which must have occurred over and over again in human history; a devoted band of pioneers, with unbounded enthusiasm and faith in their mission, feeling themselves frustrated by the caution and self-protective instincts of established enterprise. It is very understandable. The BBC accepted television in 1936, but appears not to have embraced it or fully taken it to heart until 1950 when Haley decided to promote it to a level with sound radio by appointing a Director of Television, who with five others of equal rank would be a director of the BBC and a member of the Board of Management. George Barnes (later Sir George Barnes) got the job. When I succeeded Barnes in 1956 I could still detect a remnant of the old suspicion amongst the staff—a suspicion that the sound radio tail was wagging the television dog, but I could discover no present reason for the suspicion and had little difficulty in dispelling it after a few months. The suspicion lingered on a little longer outside the BBC; Ministers and Members of Parliament used to ask me whether I thought BBC Television was being held back in anyway by its affiliation with a sound radio corporation. They seemed to expect me to say yes, but I always told them that the boot was on the other leg. I was rather ashamed of the concentration of attention on television, and was afraid that it was proving so powerful a magnet for the audience and for talent of all kinds that it might emasculate sound radio.

But to revert to the earlier situation. Most television in the world started as an extension of existing sound radio services by the addition of a second dimension. Television carried with it the certainty of considerable damage to radio, the certainty of greatly increased costs but no certainty of correspondingly increased returns; it was at the same time a disturbance and a risk. No wonder those with big stakes in radio, whether they were broadcasters or manufacturers, were reluctant to take the plunge.

CHAPTER 4

Who Controls Television?

TELEVISION is essentially a domestic medium of communication, because amongst other disabilities its range is so limited that it cannot normally be used for direct communication with the people of other countries. Television services speak to their own people almost exclusively, and unlike sound radio, which can be transmitted over very long distances, television is not an effective instrument of foreign policy. This is all to the good, because it means that television makes less mischief between governments. However, it has important international aspects of another kind, and these will be dealt with in other parts of this book.

After the initial start by Britain before the war, the United States entered the television field as soon as the war was over. In the course of time most of the European countries came in, and now (1962), less than seventeen years after the war, there are eighty countries with television in more or less developed stages. It is estimated that there are about 110,000,000 receiving sets in use, 12,000,000 in Britain, 65,000,000 in the United States, the rest distributed amongst the remaining seventy-eight countries, and thus the scope for further expansion on a colossal scale within the next few years is obvious.

I guess that somewhere between three and four hundred million people make use of television regularly, while many more come under its influence. It is estimated that the average viewer in Britain looks at television about two and a half hours a day, and in America it is much the same, while children everywhere are enthusiastic addicts. The power of this instrument to mould the minds of men is already very great; in a few decades it will be gigantic. It is no good anyone pretending that television is just a relaxing entertainment to occupy leisure hours; if it were no more than that, it would be a pleasantly harmless facility for an affluent society, but that is not how television is used in practice. There are very often ulterior motives on the part of the providers, who set themselves to mould the minds of men and women in one way or another, and it is this moulding process which needs such constant vigilance by responsible citizens in all countries. Television is an instrument through which a very small number of people can mould the minds of hundreds, perhaps thousands of millions of their fellow men, and so it is an instrument of immense political and economic power.

Television and radio differ profoundly from any of the other forms of public presentation, firstly because the number of services which can be offered in any given area is restricted by nature, therefore they are exclusive and quasi monopolistic, and a franchise to use one of the very limited number of channels is a prize of great value. (Mr. Roy Thomson once referred to it as a licence to print one's own bank notes.) Secondly television cannot collect directly from its customers the cost of the service it renders. The theatre, the circus, the stadium, printed publications of all kinds can withhold their services and so enforce payment, but broadcasting cannot. So Television and Radio do not stand on their own feet; they are in a weak position, vulnerable to exploitation, because they are dependent for their franchises and their revenue on third parties. Those third parties, because of their indispensability, are in a position to exploit the medium in their own special interests, which may not be the best interests of the people, and this is the kernel of the problem of broadcasting.

Who are the people who wield the power? How do they wield it? Where do they get the power from? The prime source of all power in broadcasting is government, which might be said in a vague sort of way about almost everything in life, but it is true in a very special and direct sense of broadcasting. The channels are natural phenomena and limited in number. It is difficult to say that anybody is able to own such insubstantial property as channels, but in fact they are public property. Each government acts as if it were the proprietor of the channels, and government can use some or all of the channels itself for a variety of purposes including broadcasting, or it can delegate the use of channels to others. It can charge big rents for the use of channels, but I do not know of any country where this is done. When a government delegates the use of channels to others, it lays down conditions as to how the channels shall be used; the conditions and above all the enforcement or nonenforcement of them control the type and quality of our broadcasting services. Governments therefore have a very special responsibility in this matter everywhere, even in the most democratic free enterprise countries, even in the United States. The only limitation on the exercise by a government of these undoubted responsibilities could be an absence of public opinion permitting obstructive influences by the elected representatives of the people; in other words pressure groups.

I shall deal in another chapter with broadcasting's Achilles Heel—finance, but here I want to make the point that governments are always responsible for choosing the broadcasters and for prescribing the methods by which they shall finance themselves, and if they are wise governments they issue regulations designed to protect the broadcasters, and through them the people, from the excessive influence of big business and of government itself. These are the two powerful influences to one or other of which broadcasting everywhere is vulnerable.

The extent of government influence, amounting in some countries to direct control, is always a matter of concern to thoughtful people in the non-communist world. Television being a domestic service only, people are rightly concerned lest it be used by their own governments as an instrument of internal political persuasion to enhance the power of the governing groups and to reduce the prospects of their rivals. That it is so used in some non-communist countries is beyond question. In this context the communist countries are hardly worth discussing, because their political philosophy, amounting as it does to a religion, does not recognize the validity of any kind of rivalry to the existing power groups. Of course in such circumstances television is controlled by government, and any other arrangement would be unthinkable. But in the non-communist world there is no standard pattern, and the degrees of government influence on television vary enormously according to the political maturity and the historical background of the country concerned. Anything short of complete government control would hardly be expected in Spain or Portugal, while in France the Director General of Radio Television Francais is not chosen, as he is in Britain from the ranks of his broadcasting colleagues. He is a government appointee, who works in a government office alongside the Minister concerned.

These things are unwelcome and disturbing to Britons and Americans, but I think we should not be too censorious of them. Both our countries have political traditions which are based on a high degree of national unity, but few other countries are so fortunate. The degree of national unity, which Britons and Americans take for granted, does not by any means apply to all other countries, and it does not surprise me in the very least to know that television is used deliberately by some governments as an instrument of internal policy to promote national unity, but the dividing line between the interests of national unity and the interests of the groups in power is one which I would not care to have to define.

I have spent a lot of time in America in recent years and especially in 1961. I have addressed so many gatherings of business, university and professional people that I have lost count of the number, and I have had innumerable conversations with Americans about broadcasting. Wherever I have been I have come across the firmly held but wholly erroneous belief that, because the main instrument of television in Britain finances itself through the agency of a government department, it is ipso facto government controlled, and that it exists primarily to promote British government policies. Our image in America is not helped by the fact that many non-commercial television organizations in other countries are in fact used in this way, and it is difficult for Americans, whose own television is quite blatantly controlled by big business, to visualize any alternative except control by government. Of the two they much prefer the former. Our government made a mistake in 1954 in allowing the newly-created British Commercial Television Authority to call itself The *Independent* Television Authority. The adjective was intended to imply its independence of the BBC which was factually correct, but outside Britain, and especially in America, it was taken to mean independence of the government, with the inevitable implication that the BBC, the 'Main Instrument' of British television, was not independent of the government and was indeed an instrument of government policy, which most Americans were predisposed to believe anyway. This mistaken image is further encouraged by the well-known fact that Britain's external sound radio services are a part of the BBC's normal operations, while equivalent operations in America are wholly controlled by a department of the Federal Government.

The independence enjoyed by the BBC, and incidentally by the ITA too, is something which is difficult for foreigners to grasp, but when they do grasp it they admire it enormously. It is one of Britain's more important assets and it is a pity to make understanding more difficult than it need be by the careless use of titles. When I was speaking to a French audience in Paris in the spring of 1961 I found some incredulity and much admiration for the BBC's high degree of freedom from Government control.

The United States of America is the foreign country I know best, especially in television terms. As in every other country, the supreme authority in American broadcasting is the central government, which exercises its authority through a body known as the Federal Communications Commission in Washington. The chairman of the Commission is a brilliant young lawyer named Newton Minow, who is the most outstanding and controversial figure in the business. The Commission, acting for the Federal Government, regulates the use of the available channels and decides who shall use them and how they shall use them; thus the Commission, in respect of broadcasting, has much the same functions and powers as our Postmaster General, issuing licences to station owners and prescribing the type of programming permitted under the licences.

This would seem to be a perfectly simple and straightforward state of affairs, but in fact it is very far from straightforward. The licences permit the station owners to use the public channels, and in return the owners are expected to provide public services worthy of the American people, but in America they overlook the fact that, unless the Federal Government provides the facilities, the station owners have no means of collecting revenue from their customers, and they are left with no alternative but to hire out their air time to business corporations, most of whom have not the slightest interest in providing public services worthy of the American people. In this matter the Federal Government is like a father who makes heavy social demands on his daughters without providing them with a penny piece or assisting them in any way to earn an honest living. To survive, let alone be social successes, they must sell their only saleable asset—themselves, and, if father objects, he is not being quite reasonable.

On May 9, 1961, shortly after his appointment, Newton Minow addressed the annual convention of the National Association of Broadcasters in Washington. Here are a few of the more significant sentences, which I have extracted from the text of the speech:

'You earn your bread by using public property.'

'Your licence lets you use the public's airwaves as trustees for 180,000,000 Americans.'

'As a representative of the public, your health and your product are among my chief concerns.'

'I have confidence in your health. But not in your product.'

'If he (the Chairman of the Association who had made the previous speech) meant that we intend to enforce the law in the public interest, let me make it perfectly clear that he is right— we do. If he meant that we intend to muzzle or censor broadcasting, he is dead wrong.'

'Your industry possesses the most powerful voice in America. It has an inescapable duty to make that voice ring with intelligence and leadership.'

'I invite you to sit down in front of your television set when your station goes on the air . . . and keep your eyes glued to that set till the station signs off. I can assure you you will observe a vast wasteland.'

'Gentlemen your trust accounting with your beneficiaries is overdue.'

'Never have so few owed so much to so many.'

This is powerful stuff, and it comes from the man who is the trustee for the owners of the channels—the American people. He is saying, on behalf of his people, that their channels are not being properly used by those to whom the Commission has entrusted their use. I offer no opinion as to whether Minow's judgement is right or wrong, but he has a very firm conviction and the question arises—what is he going to do about it? The more one looks into the matter the more difficult it appears for Minow to do anything effective, except to arouse public opinion by making speeches like this.

The Americans are so afraid of concentrations of power that no one is allowed to own more than five television stations and seven radio stations, and as the country has about five thousand radio stations and over five hundred television stations, it follows that the owners are numerous and the broadcasting lobby is correspondingly large. It is a very formidable pressure group; some extremely powerful people own television stations. I did a broadcast from a television station in Arizona and was informed by the manager that the station was owned by the wife of the Vice-President of the United States, and a recent US Ambassador to the Court of St James once told me he owned a number of television stations in America. That Minow is up against a hostile and powerful lobby in Congress is a well-known fact.

He talks about enforcing the law, but that means taking legal action against station owners who, in the Commission's opinion, are not broadcasting good enough programmes. The quality and standard of programming can so easily be held to be a matter of opinion, and what about the evidence? Whose evidence on such insubstantial matters would a judge accept?

The commission has no jurisdiction over network operations, only over the operations of individual stations, which is a grave handicap to it. I believe that the only real weapon in the Commission's armoury is the power to refuse to renew a station licence after it has expired, and it will be very interesting to see whether this weapon is in fact used, more especially against the bigger game.

Meanwhile the spokesmen for the television interests do not remain silent; Mr Robert Sarnoff, chairman of the board of the National Broadcasting Company of America which controls the senior network in the United States, has forcibly defended the citadel; so has Dr Frank Stanton, President of the Columbia Broadcasting System, another giant. Dr Stanton has been kind enough to send me a reprint of his Benjamin Franklin Lecture at the University of Pennsylvania on December 7, 1961, in the course of which he referred to Mr Minow's recommendation to view a whole day's programmes from any one station resulting, in Minow's opinion, in the impression of a 'vast wasteland'. This is Stanton's rejoinder:

'The danger of this sensationalized and over-simplified approach, with its broad brush conclusions, is not only that it grotesquely distorts the situation as it is, a clear perception of which is necessary to improvement, but also that it invites impulsive measures directed at making fundamental changes on the ground that any change is a change for the better. Actually the only change that I have seen suggested is that the government supervise programming by the use of its licensing powers and by regulating a major programme source, the networks.

How much improvement can either of these really bring about? If government authority sets standards, qualitative and quantitative, for television programming, whose standards are they going to be? The chairman of a commission? A majority of a commission? A congressional committee?

You would have authoritative standards that would stifle creativity. You would have a rigidity that would discourage experimentation. You would have the subjective judgment of a small group imposed on the many. *And you would have the constant danger of the misuse of the medium for political purposes.*' (My italics.)

Dr. Stanton then went on to quote Justice Brandies.

'Experience should teach us to be most on our guard to protect liberty when the government's purposes are beneficent. Men born to freedom are naturally alert to repel invasion of their liberty by evil-minded rulers. The greatest dangers to liberty lurk in insidious encroachments by men of zeal . . .'

This is a magnificent defence of that most cherished of all American ideals—liberty. It is the kind of defence that the BBC might put up if it were threatened with the sort of situation which exists in French broadcasting, but the BBC (and to a large extent the ITA also) is in a totally different position from American broadcasting, because it always has liberty to defend—it is controlled by neither government nor big business; it really is master in its own house.

I agree wholeheartedly with Dr Stanton that anything in the nature of editorial control of programmes by government would be a very retrograde step, and I happen to know that it is the last thing Mr Minow wants. I agree with Dr Stanton in his passionate desire for freedom for those engaged in broadcasting, freedom from irresistible pressures (e.g. sponsors) which divert broadcasters from their plain duty to the public, but American television has little liberty to defend; it has yet to acquire liberty.

Abstract appeals for liberty are always exciting but seldom satisfying, because they beg too many questions. Whose liberty? Liberty of what? Liberty for what? How much liberty? The emotional response to an appeal for liberty usually derives from the innate love of personal and individual liberty which is so strong in Western man, especially in those of the Anglo-Saxon tradition, but what liberty does the individual viewer enjoy in terms of television? He has the liberty of the switch and that is just about all; he has the liberty to take or leave what somebody else chooses to give him. Television is valuable to the individual in many ways, but it confers no liberty on him. When we speak of liberty in television, we can mean only one thing—liberty for those who provide the programmes, freedom from the incubus of government and sponsor alike, liberty to give of their best to the viewer without the distortions of governmental or industrial politics. Television's inability to finance itself without the aid of government or industry makes it extremely difficult for it to achieve and protect its essential liberties.

Some human societies are bedevilled by an excess of dogmatic ideology, where a useful notion becomes magnified into a kind of religion, and human activities, whatever their nature, tend to be squeezed into the ideological pattern. For instance in Russia and China agriculture has to conform to the Marxist pattern, but agriculture is a kind of activity which is most productive under a system of relatively free private enterprise. The enormous productivity of American and European agriculture is in remarkable contrast to the consistently disappointing results of agriculture in communist countries. On the other hand television is not by nature free private enterprise, and to squeeze it into that mould for ideological reasons is to rob it of its liberty and render it liable to exploitation.

The basic problem of television everywhere is how to secure its essential freedoms in spite of its financial dependence, and the countries which come nearest to solving this problem are the countries where television has the best opportunity to develop its full potential in the public interest.

But freedom can never be absolute; freedom for television is in the gift of the sovereign power and it can be preserved only by the sovereign power. Government cannot escape the full responsibility for the television services within its own frontiers. It is government alone which has the power to grant or withhold franchises, to lay down conditions and to enforce fulfilment of the conditions. It is government alone which can protect television against exploitation by others and against exploitation by government itself. Television differs from most other forms of enterprise, which thrive best on a minimum of government intervention. Television does not; it was not 'born to freedom'; it has no inherent freedom; it must be given freedom, protected in that freedom; and held to its job of serving the public interest.

The state of American television is a matter of the greatest possible concern to everybody in the industry whether they be American or not, because a very high proportion (some put it at fifty per cent or more) of all television programmes shown throughout the non-communist world are American programmes, the Westerns, the private eyes, and the situation comedies, with some of which British audiences are familiar. They form the principal diet of viewers of all races and colours in a majority of the eighty countries which have television, but they are made specifically for the American market, which therefore holds the key to their nature and their quality. Somebody or some small group decides what shall be shown to the American people, and whoever makes the decision wields (unwittingly no doubt) immense power not only in America but throughout the free world. Who makes the decision? It is widely believed that the sponsor does it; the manufacturer of soap, cigarettes, canned foods, beer or some other consumer product. In a great many cases no doubt the sponsor leaves it to his advertising agent, whose choice is made with regard to the business interests of the sponsoring corporation, though he may also have to consider the private political, social or religious views of the sponsor. He is not normally called upon to have regard for the interests of the American people let alone the interests of the world-wide audiences who will be shown the programmes because he has chosen them.

But this is not quite the whole story, because the owners of the television stations are responsible in law for what is broadcast, and they cannot legally delegate that responsibility to a sponsor or anyone else. The networks for instance have 'Acceptance' departments who carry that responsibility, but unless some major matter of principle is at stake, it would seem normal to let the sponsor have his way; after all he pays.

I have been fortunate enough to meet a few of the biggest American sponsors and to get their views, and I have done the same with some of the larger advertising agents. It is quite clear to me that the sponsor does not always have it entirely his own way, though he would like to, and it appears that the networks are sometimes a bit tough. There is not a complete identity of interests between the two parties. I was once told, quite seriously, by one advertising agent that the American government ought to prohibit the television industry from having any finger at all in the programme producing pie. This was suggested as a measure to prevent them from trying to force upon sponsors filmed programmes in which the television people themselves had financial interests, and it was alleged that this practice, by yielding an extra source of profit to the television people, gave rise to pressures which interfered with the sponsor's freedom of choice.

The question, who in fact directly controls American programming and thereby indirectly the bulk of the world's programming, is not an easy one to answer. The power seems to lie in a somewhat uneasy compromise between the big manufacturing and commercial corporations on the one hand and the television networks on the other, but it is a state of affairs in which it is difficult to detect much in the way of freedom for the broadcasters to serve the public interest.

If this were a purely internal American problem, it would be impertinent of me, a foreigner, to criticize it, but in fact it concerns everybody in the non-communist world and particularly the less developed countries of Asia and Africa. America is the dominant factor and to a large extent the peoples of the world are in her hands, especially in television entertainment, because only the very rich countries can afford to make their own on anything like the required scale. For economic reasons the rest must accept whatever American big business chooses to send them.

CHAPTER 5

Money

BROADCASTING to earn its keep must use either government or industry as its collecting agent. One of the British networks uses government, the other uses industry, and I shall give some account in this chapter of the finances of the two networks. Before doing so, I want to draw attention to the fairly widespread use outside Britain of gifts or subsidies for television.

In so far as television accepts gifts or subsidies, it fails to earn its own living, but gifts and subsidies are sometimes offered as inducements to make television do something useful, which it would not do of its own accord. The failure of American commercial television to provide sufficient educational material has given rise to the subsidization of about sixty educational stations by various foundations, universities and other benefactors. In Canada, where the commercialization of television has been allowed to get out of hand, the Government subsidizes the Canadian Broadcasting Corporation to the tune of about $52,000,000 a year in order to preserve a Canadian element in the programmes and to provide employment for Canadian artists. Otherwise Canadian television would be little more than a shop window for American goods and American talent. The fear of degradation by commercialism prompted our own government at one time to offer a subsidy to the ITA to improve the balance of its programmes, but the ITA was prevented from accepting it by the opposition of its own programme companies. It is an odd fact that commercial television, which is so expensive for the customer and so profitable for its operators, seems to give rise to still further expenditure from public and private sources in attempts to correct its deficiencies.

In Britain there has never been any subsidization, public or private, of domestic broadcasting. The BBC has never been offered, nor sought, any kind of subsidy, and has relied entirely on its earnings from licence revenue augmented to a small extent by profits on the sale of its publications and television programmes. British experience of the licence system is important, because this is the country of its birth, and from here it spread to the continent and became the traditional European system of broadcasting finance. It is the cheapest system from the customer's point of view and it generally produces the best results, but it has one inherent danger. Governments are not immune from the temptation of profits; the payment of licence fees cannot be enforced unless the fees have the legal status of taxes, and taxes can be pocketed by the government and treated as ordinary state revenue. Then broadcasting is left with only two alternatives—commercialization or state subsidy, or a mixture of both as in Canada, and in either case broadcasting loses its liberty and its programmes deteriorate.

That this danger is no idle supposition can be shown by reference to the sixth report of the British Committee of Public Accounts published in July, 1956:

'The present method of financing the Corporation (the BBC) under binding agreements for years ahead, although neither future income nor future expenditure can be closely estimated, seems to your Committee to be open to objection. They accordingly recommend that this method should be reviewed, licence fees should be regarded strictly as revenue from taxation and the annual grants which Parliament is asked to provide should not be in excess of the sums that the Government are satisfied the Corporation will require in the particular years concerned. This would bring the arrangements into line with the normal system of Parliamentary grants to bodies which have some independent income. They also recommend that grants should be split into separate heads for capital development and current expenditure.' (Paragraph 30.)

If this recommendation had been accepted, the licence system as a method by which broadcasting earns its living would have been thrown out of the window; the special contribution of the British, so much admired and widely copied elsewhere, would have been scrapped in the country of its birth. Fortunately the

MONEY

Treasury turned it down in no uncertain terms:

'Their Lordships have carefully considered the recommendations of the Committee in paragraph 30 of their report that the grants to the Corporation should cease to be paid in pursuance of binding agreements which, in effect, allocate licence revenue between the Exchequer and the Corporation over a period of years. They are not persuaded, however, that any change in this long-standing arrangement is either necessary or desirable. The existing system, which has been endorsed by successive Committees of Enquiry over the years, is sufficiently flexible to obviate excessive accumulations of reserves by the Corporation over long periods. At the same time it enables the Corporation to plan ahead and preserves the independence the Corporation has always had in the day-to-day conduct of its business. In the opinion of Their Lordships it would be undesirable to break the link between licence revenue and the annual grants to the Corporation.' (Treasury Minute. February 7, 1957.)

This showed an understanding of the problem, but had their Lordships accepted the committee's recommendation to divorce licence revenue from the Corporation's income it would have been nothing short of a disaster. The reader may be puzzled by the Treasury's way of referring to the BBC's income (or 'earnings' as I prefer to call it) as 'annual grants', which seems like the terminology of subsidy and for that reason it is a great pity that it should be used in this context. The annual grant by Parliament is, in effect, a fiction intended to provide Parliament with an annual opportunity of discussing the BBC, which in itself is an excellent thing, but the implication that the BBC lives by subsidies from general taxation is misleading and damaging to the prestige of British broadcasting at home and abroad.

The Post Office collects the revenue from the customers, and withholds a sum which is intended to reimburse the Post Office for the costs of collection, for investigating complaints of electrical interference, and administrative expenses. Having deducted this sum the balance is known as the 'net licence revenue'.

The BBC's current 'Licence and Agreement' with the Post

master General dated the twelfth of June, 1952, states that the Postmaster General will for three years pay over to the BBC eighty-five per cent of the net licence revenue. Thereafter he will pay over to the BBC 'a sum equal to such percentage or percentages of the net licence revenue as the Treasury may authorize.'

Several important things arise out of this. The BBC's earnings are (or were till the ITA came along) wholly dependent on the acceptability of its products and directly linked with it. The proportion of the net licence revenue due to the BBC is settled by the Treasury for several years ahead, generally three, and any downward alteration by Parliament of the agreed proportion would create chaos in the BBC. The Treasury is the body with which the BBC has to negotiate to secure for itself the highest possible percentage. The BBC does not in any circumstances get more than its total earnings, which would be 100% of the net licence revenue, but if it did, it would be receiving a subsidy.

It is an interesting exercise to translate all this into normal business terms. In 1927 the State bought the business of the British Broadcasting Company Ltd at par, which was £71,000, and this is the State's total investment in the BBC. The State thereafter became in effect the sole shareholder, and as shareholder the State is represented by the Treasury. The BBC has been a very lucrative business; the profits on trading account have been enormous in relation to the investment, so large that all subsequent capital development has been financed out of them. The governors and directors of the BBC have always sought to plough the profits back into the business on the fullest practical scale so as to develop it as rapidly as possible, and they have wanted to carry liquid reserves against future developments. But the shareholder has not taken quite the same view and, like so many shareholders, has favoured a generous distribution of profits. (In this case it is the shareholder who has the last word on the size of the dividend.) In fact the total sum distributed to the State between the end of the war and April, 1961, was about £28,000,000. This sum represents the dividends paid over fifteen years on an investment of £71,000.

Of course there are a number of respects in which the BBC cannot properly be equated with an ordinary trading firm, but this little exercise is useful because it shows that in the BBC the State has a highly profitable business, and one which has made a large contribution to the national exchequer since the end of the war.

I am frequently asked, especially in America, about the extent of the Government's control over the BBC, and while I am always able to say that in practice its control over day-to-day management and over editorial matters is nil, I have to admit that the Government does exercise a broad financial control, which in turn governs the pace of the BBC's development and the scope of its activities, and this control could be very irksome and frustrating. It has never been a part of my own duties to negotiate with the Treasury officials, but I have always understood from my colleagues that they are very reasonable men and carry out sympathetically and intelligently the policies of the Government in relation to the BBC. A good understanding between the Treasury and the BBC is essential.

However, the controlling hand is there and the question arises as to whether it is used wisely. It certainly was used in the decade after the war to hold the BBC's development back, and at the time of the debates about commercial television the BBC was unfairly accused of going slow in a number of respects. It is not for me to say whether the 'go slow' was necessary in the national interest, but I do know that it put the BBC in a weak position at a time when it needed all its strength. The situation began to unfreeze in the mid-nineteen fifties, and the then Director General, Sir Ian Jacob, a doughty fighter and a bold spender, took the fullest advantage of the easing position and pressed forward with the development of the television service. But the fact remains that much of what has now been achieved could have been achieved much earlier if the BBC had not been held back by government policy.

The question of reserves is raised both in the report of the Public Accounts Committee and in the Treasury minute, and the reader will note that both bodies seem to disapprove of the BBC having substantial reserves. I have never been able to follow this argument unless it be to limit the financial independence of the BBC. The reserves would not lie idle; they would add to the nation's invested capital, but now the BBC, because so much of its post-war trading profit has been retained by the Treasury, will be substantially in the red before the end of the extended charter period. (No adequate financial provision was made for the extra two years added to the Charter period at a late stage.) If the BBC had been allowed to retain its post-war trading profits this would not have arisen. It now faces the prospect of a second BBC television network and important developments in sound radio, especially in local broadcasting, but the absence of a big reserve means that none of these things can be achieved without an increase in the licence fee. Some increase would have been needed anyway, but it is obvious that, had the profits been kept in the business, these further developments could have been financed at a lower price to the customer, that is to say a smaller licence fee, than in fact will be necessary now, and it seems to me that to some extent the customer is being made to pay twice over.

Today the so-called 'Television Licence' costs the customer £4 per annum, but only half this sum is for the television licence. The other half is divided equally between BBC sound radio and the Inland Revenue Department. The latter collects a £1 tax on every household with television just as it collects 7/6 on every dog. If we must be taxed, it seems to me that television viewing is as fair a thing to tax as whisky, dogs, tobacco or sweets, but it is important to remember that the tax is no part of the BBC's licence revenue.

At the time of writing there are about twelve and a half million television licences and so the gross television revenue is about twenty-five million pounds a year. Since April, 1961, the Treasury has not retained any of it, so the BBC is now getting the full net revenue. During the next two years, until the present Charter expires, there will be some increase in the total number of licences, but the increase will not be sufficient to cover the rising cost of the television service, and so the BBC will have to borrow money, and pay it back later.

The logicality of the licence system was never in dispute so long as the BBC was the sole broadcasting authority, but the advent of ITA has upset the logic. It is now possible to argue that somebody might buy a television set with the sole object of viewing the ITA. Indeed one defaulter when sued by the Post Office, claimed that he was in that position; he stuck to his point and went to jail, but this sort of thing is so rare as to have no real validity. (Many people who never look at ITA, because they can't, nevertheless help to pay for commercial television through the goods they buy, and this is even more illogical.)

The finances of British commercial television are much more involved than those of the BBC and information is less accessible to the general public. The total picture is an amalgam of the statutory body (the ITA) and its fourteen contracting programme companies. The ITA, taken by itself, is simple. It owns and operates all the transmitting stations and rents from the Post Office the interconnecting links. It owns and operates the network, which costs money; otherwise ITA's expenses are very small. It makes a rental charge to each contracting company for the use of one or more of the transmitters and this is ITA's sole source of income. The authority's last annual report and accounts for the year 1960-61 disclosed an operating income of £4,212,517, which much more than covered its operating costs. A note by the authority published with its 1958-59 report states:

'The payments made by the companies to the Authority under the contracts between them are of an order that fully complies with the ample discharge of all these responsibilities, and in fact, at the end of the period 1954-1964, the Authority
1. will have no debt to the Exchequer
2. will have acquired from income, and so hold free of debt, capital assets, mainly in the form of television transmitting stations, of the total first cost of £5,000,000, on which depreciation of some £2,750,000 will have been provided
3. will hold in revenue reserves some £4,000,000, unless further responsibilities . . . are placed on it . . .
4. will have paid in taxation a total of some £7,000,000.

These very substantial assets will, in 1964, vest in the Crown, in default of statutory provision to the contrary.'

There was a time when the Public Accounts Committee expressed the view that the authority was not charging high enough rentals to its companies and that the contracts should have been put out to competitive tender, but the authority denied both. No doubt the Committee was feeling that some of the vast profits being made by the companies should be syphoned off into the exchequer via the ITA, but the ITA took the view that 'the Act does not require the Authority to provide itself with an income out of which sums in addition to income tax should be paid to the exchequer, though it would have been possible for Parliament to add such an obligation to those defined in Section 10 had such been its wish.' Furthermore the authority 'has in no case invited competitive tenders, nor would it ever wish, by so doing, to create the impression, or leave any ground for the suggestion, that factors other than those of qualifications and suitability in relation to the provision of programmes could influence its judgment.'

ITA seems to be in a very satisfactory financial position. It is not profiteering for the exchequer. On the other hand it is building up, at no cost to the taxpayer, a public asset in the shape of a national television network. The real nub of commercial television finance is with the contracting companies, who, after incurring very large losses in the first two years, turned the corner, recovered their losses and began to make huge profits, which are now regarded by many people as excessive. I find it difficult to agree with the critics. The risks in the early stages were great and the contracts were for limited periods; the companies have been lucky, but they might have been unlucky; they took a chance and they won; the stakes were high and the rewards are correspondingly high. The fault lies, not with the companies, but with the 1954 Parliament.

It is much more difficult to get a clear view of the financial position of the companies, because they, especially the big four, have many other interests, which lie outside television proper; nor is it known to me how much of the revenue from television advertising is spent on television programmes. However, it is possible to make some sort of an estimate of their total advertising revenue, and of the total cost of their television. (The latter can only be very rough.) The latest published figures indicate that their advertising revenue is running at the rate of about £110,000,000 a year, out of which is paid the special tax of eleven per cent recently imposed on television advertising. The cost of their television service cannot be very substantially higher than the cost of the BBC's television service, which is of the order of £25,000,000 a year including all administrative and capital expenditure. It may be a little higher, because the

MONEY

ITA do not do quite so much networking as the BBC, but their overall hours of transmission are the same. I should not be surprised to find that the ratio of advertising revenue to television expenditure was about four to one. I have no knowledge of what they spend on television. I only know that a first-rate nation-wide television service of about sixty hours a week can be had for roughly £25,000,000 a year. So the margin of profit is high, which accounts for the high dividends, the bonus issues and the high value of the shares on the stock market.

The most important consideration of all is the price which the customer pays for his television services. I will discuss this matter in relation to the individual householder, the man or woman who pays the household expenses. Let us suppose there are seventeen million of them, three-quarters of whom have television, and between them all they have to find the £110,000,000 and another £7,000,000 to cover the cost of making the advertisements. If we deduct the eleven per cent tax, we are still left with a figure of over £100,000,000 which has to be paid by the 17,000,000 households to maintain the ITA network. They pay it through the goods they buy in the shops, and it averages about £6 a year for each household, irrespective of whether they have television or not. The price of the BBC network is £2 a year for each household with television; nothing for households without television.

There might be some justification for this very big difference in price if the ITA network were markedly more acceptable to the public than the BBC network, but in fact this is not so. There is very little difference between the two networks in terms of public acceptability; for many months the average ratio has been in the neighbourhood of 50:50. So we must look for some justification other than public acceptability. It may be that the nation's economy would run down or fail to expand if we had no commercial television; perhaps we are all better off, and enjoying a higher standard of living, because we have commercial television. I shall consider these matters in a later chapter on television advertising.

CHAPTER 6

The Liberty of British Television

IN Britain we have two television networks, both State owned. This statement may come as a surprise to some of my readers, because one of the networks conducts its programme operations through contractors who are not State owned. Public attention is directed by publicity towards the contractors, and so people are apt to overlook the fact that the ITA's network is the property of the State; it is in fact a creation of the State. The BBC, though not a creation of the State, was acquired for the State by purchase from its original owners. Both are now public property, and constitutionally they have much in common. Both are governed by authorities, whose individual members are publicly appointed by the State for defined and limited periods of office; both authorities are answerable to Parliament and in fact make annual reports to Parliament through the Postmaster General; both operate under terms of reference designed by Government and approved by Parliament; both are subject to certain overt Government powers of control over the content of their programmes, both have powers to produce their own programmes.

But they part company in two very important ways. The ITA is not intended, except in abnormal circumstances, to produce its own programmes, while the BBC is. The ITA is instructed, whenever practicable, to contract out of programme production. There is nothing to stop the BBC from contracting out for individual programmes or series of programmes, but it *is* not intended that the BBC should employ 'Programme Contractors' as defined in the Television Act of 1954. Thus the ITA is an authority and an exhibitor, while the BBC is an authority, an exhibitor and a *producer*.

The second and more important difference is the financial

difference. The BBC lives on an agreed proportion of the licence revenue and is forbidden to broadcast advertisements. The ITA is permitted to broadcast advertisements and is expected to live on rentals derived from the advertising revenue collected by its 'Programme Contractors'.

This chapter is about liberty. To what extent, if at all, does this state of affairs inhibit the liberty of the two authorities? I have said that in both cases the Government reserves certain overt powers of control over the content of programmes, and I will revert to these powers later. Meanwhile I refer to other forms of power or influence which could inhibit the liberty of the authorities to serve the best interests of the public. The BBC directly controls its own programming, but the ITA does not. Its control is through its long-term contracts and through certain powers vested in it by the Act. In this respect BBC enjoys more liberty than ITA. The BBC's revenue is not directly dependent on the size of its audience, while the ITA contractor's revenue is directly dependent on it. So here again the BBC enjoys more liberty to serve the best interests of the public.

On the other hand the BBC derives its revenue through the agency of a government department—the Post Office. This gives the Government a financial hold over the BBC which can be used to hold back development, and in this respect the ITA and its contractors enjoy more liberty than the BBC does.

To what extent, if at all, are the editorial liberties of the two authorities undermined by the demands of the Government and the requirements of the advertisers? These are the two danger points. I deal with the advertisers first. The BBC broadcasts no advertisements and is not therefore amenable to advertising pressure of any kind. The ITA is prohibited from having any of its programmes sponsored by advertisers, and is permitted only to sell advertising time in the intervals between programmes and in natural breaks. No advertiser is allowed any influence at all on the editorial policy of ITA or on the nature of its programmes, but one must not overlook the fact that for the ITA the advertiser is the customer, and he needs large, steady, predictable audiences for his advertisements. Nobody particularly wants to look at advertisements, so the audiences have to be attracted and held by the surrounding programmes, which are the bait on the advertiser's hook. This is an unfortunate necessity of all commercial television. It does in practice constitute an infringement of the liberty of the authority to serve the best interests of the public, because it compels an over-emphasis on entertainment and a corresponding under-emphasis on education, and this has always been the principal criticism of the ITA's service. That the ITA itself may be aware of it is suggested by its advocacy of a separate educational network to make up for the inevitable unbalance of commercial television.

The government has power under the BBC's licence from the Postmaster General and under the Act setting up the ITA to instruct either authority to broadcast or to refrain from broadcasting something specific or some particular class of material. If these powers were widely exercised they could result in government control over the day-to-day editorial policy of both authorities. In fact they are hardly exercised at all. The Government, in time of peace, has never exercised anything approaching editorial control. It has used its power four times and then only to give general instructions of a kind which might well be issued by the Federal Communication Commission in America to its licence-holders. These are the four instructions:

1. That the BBC must be politically impartial. (Still in force.)
2. That the BBC must not be controversial. (Rescinded in 1928.)
3. That neither authority must mount discussions of important issues within fourteen days before their being debated in Parliament. (Rescinded after a few months.)
4. That party political broadcasts must be balanced in relation to the United Kingdom as a whole and not in relation to particular regions. (Still in force).

Apart from 2 and 3, which were ill-advised and quickly rescinded, it can be said that the Government's powers have never been used to the detriment of either authority, and in practice they have never been a threat to editorial liberty. There is one important safeguard against their being so used; both BBC and ITA are authorized to announce publicly that they are broadcasting or refraining from broadcasting something on government instructions. So the government cannot use its powers secretly, and any instruction given by government is open to comment and criticism by Parliament and Press.

I have always believed that, far from constituting a threat to liberty, these formal overt governmental powers are a positive safeguard of liberty, because in the absence of such powers it might be very difficult for the authorities to resist governmental pressures exercised secretly. If a government hasn't the formal power to instruct, its wishes and strongly expressed desires may easily become irresistible pressures, but, the formal powers being there, government's wishes can be resisted if in the opinion of either broadcasting authority they are ill-advised. To get its way the Government only has to instruct openly and the responsibility for the decision becomes theirs.

I do not believe there is a country in the world where the broadcasting authorities are more free of government interference with programmes than they are in Britain. An example may be useful to the reader. In the early stages of the Suez crisis in 1956 the Prime Minister, Sir Anthony Eden (now Lord Avon), broadcast a talk to the British people on BBC television and sound radio. He was to have spoken as Prime Minister, but after the broadcast Mr Hugh Gaitskell, the leader of the Opposition, claimed that the Prime Minister had gone beyond what was intended and had introduced matters which were of a controversial party nature. He demanded the right of reply, and he was told that, if the Prime Minister agreed, he would be given the opportunity to reply on the following night. The Prime Minister did not agree. I suppose he thought the situation was too serious for internal controversies of this sort; so the BBC was faced with an acute difference of opinion between government and opposition about the propriety of a BBC broadcast. Under the terms of the BBC's licence the Government had the power to prevent the broadcast by issuing an instruction, but it did not do so, and the decision lay with the BBC, which decided that Mr. Gaitskell had a case and invited him to express it. He made a very critical attack the following night and this was broadcast by the BBC in spite of the known wishes of the Prime Minister. I think this incident illustrates the self-confidence of the British broadcasting authorities and the boldness with which they exercise their liberties. The BBC acted as the mouthpiece, not of the Government which naturally wanted all the support it could get both at home and abroad, but of the British people who were deeply divided on the Suez issue. It also illustrates an admirable self-restraint on the part of a government, which felt itself in a very grave difficulty. It is this kind of self-restraint in the use of power, which lies at the root of democracy as we understand it in Britain.

Another important element in the liberty of British broadcasting is the exclusive power vested in the authorities to appoint their own staffs. In a highly centralized system like the BBC's the Director General necessarily wields great influence, and the power to make and unmake directors general very nearly amounts to the power of control over broadcasting. Similar appointments in some other countries are made by government. For instance it was announced a short time ago that M. Janot the Director General of Radio Television Francais had gone because of a disagreement with his Minister. In Britain he could only go because of a disagreement with his broadcasting authority—his employers; the Government would have no part in the matter.

The liberties of British broadcasting were not brought about by a single act of will, but by a chain of circumstances which constitute the history of the BBC. Professor Asa Briggs is writing that history in four volumes under the title of *History of Broadcasting in the United Kingdom*, the first volume of which is already published, and is worthy of close study by anyone who wants to know how these liberties came about. The most important influence of all was that of John Reith, who, in spite of enormous difficulties and a lot of press criticism, created confidence in the BBC's determination and ability to use broadcasting wholly in the public interest. Perhaps his greatest single triumph was his handling of the General Strike in 1926, when the BBC was almost the only means of internal communication. The temptation for the Government to take over the BBC and control its broadcasts must have been very strong. They had the power to do it in a national emergency, but by then Reith had built up such confidence in the BBC's integrity and sense of responsibility that its liberties were respected.

After forty years the liberty of broadcasting has become a

national habit—part of the political climate of our country. Habits, climates of opinion are more potent even than charters or acts of parliament. This particular climate of opinion is a wholly good one, and we must preserve it at all costs. It depends in the last resort on the quality of the men and women engaged in broadcasting, and on the public's confidence in their motives and their ability. It depends on the recognition that they are devoted exclusively to serving the best interests of the people. ITA has inherited the climate, deriving great benefit from it.

CHAPTER 7

Monopoly and Competition

PUBLIC discussions on broadcasting during the last forty years have nearly always led to arguments about monopoly. People who understand broadcasting know that it is a monopolistic activity by nature; there is nothing anyone can do to make it otherwise, and the only problem has been how to arrange matters so that the dangers, real or imaginary, of monopoly are avoided. In the early nineteen twenties, when the introduction of broadcasting into Britain was under way, it was held by the Post Office that the British Broadcasting Company was not a monopoly; it was a device for avoiding monopoly. The argument went something like this. There is room for only a limited number of stations (eight in those days), therefore there can be no more than eight concessionaires, each enjoying a monopoly in his own service area. Everyone else would be excluded from any participation in the broadcasting business. This was the sort of monopoly which the BBC was designed to avoid. The BBC was formed, largely at the instigation of the Postmaster General, as a kind of consortium of all the interested parties, who in those days were members of the radio industry. Membership of the BBC, which meant ownership of shares in the BBC, was thrown open to every bona fide member of the British radio industry. Thus, it was argued, nobody had a monopoly; everybody had an interest, and so the BBC was not a monopoly. It was a device which prevented the more powerful people, particularly the Marconi Company, from having it all their own way, but it was an odd use of the word 'monopoly'. Very soon the BBC under Reith's leadership became a more powerful entity than any of its constituent members, and, even if the BBC was not a monopoly, it unquestionably *had* a monopoly of British broadcasting. When the State acquired the BBC in 1927, nobody

MONOPOLY AND COMPETITION

any longer pretended that it was not a monopoly; it never had a right to the sole licence, but in practice successive governments, by refraining from licensing anyone else, kept the BBC as the sole instrument of British broadcasting until 1954. By licensing ITA in that year the Government set up a second quasi-monopoly for television only, and so for the first time in its history the BBC found itself sharing its audience with an authorized British competitor. (There had been fairly heavy competition for sound audiences from Radio Luxembourg for many years before 1954, but that was rather different.)

The interminable argument about monopoly in broadcasting always seems rather unreal to me. The real argument is about the desirability or otherwise of creating two or more authorities, independent of one another, to share the limited field and thereby compete with each other for the available audience. Those who have favoured this course in the past have believed that broadcasting services are subject to the simple law of supply and demand like any other commodity; that, if the people are given a free choice between two broadcasting services, they will inevitably favour the *better* of the two, and the other, finding itself losing audiences, will be stimulated to improvement by imitating the *better* features of the more favoured service. Thus standards will *rise* to a degree which could not be achieved without competition. This argument when applied to most commodities and services is a valid one. It lies at the root of free private enterprise, and the nineteenth century capitalist system, and it is a philosophy in which I was heavily indoctrinated in my youth. It is based on the presupposition that the *best* is what the people accept most readily; the customer is always right; he knows better than the supplier what is best. In a great many cases I believe this to be true; indeed, if most of us did not believe it, we ought to scrap our present economic system and try something else. But can it be applied to broadcasting? There are many of us who feel very strongly that, while most things can and should be left to the judgment of the customer, broadcasting is an exception.

We believe that broadcasting should cover such a wide range of subject matter, much of it outside the restricted experience of the average customer and some of it in advance of his powers of appreciation, that he is not in all matters fit to decide what is best. If the judgment of a majority of customers is accepted as the sole criterion, the standard of the broadcasting service will be low. This has always been the predominating philosophy of the BBC, but it is by no means confined to the BBC, it is a strongly-held belief amongst large numbers of responsible people everywhere. It is a belief that is growing stronger every day in America, where experience supports it.

But some people go further and say that competition between rival broadcasters is positively evil because far from raising standards it always lowers them. Competition in broadcasting means little more than competition for audiences, and to be successful you must be guided solely by the limited and often faulty judgment of the majority of the customers, because if you don't you will lose the race. Therefore competition between rival broadcasters is bad and should not be permitted. John Reith held this view very strongly when he was the BBC's Director General. He is often quoted as once having used the expression 'the brute force of monopoly' to describe the means without which it would have been impossible to establish a high standard of programming in the BBC. It is still the view of the BBC.

I agree that complete and unbridled competition for audiences is disastrous to standards. You can see it happening wherever in the world there are competing commercial systems. The profitability and even the solvency of a commercial station or network depends absolutely on keeping its audience 'rating' high, and if the audience rating falls the advertising revenue falls too; so every device is used to keep the rating up. Experience proves that *in the short term*, entertainment produces higher ratings than programmes which demand thought; therefore survival in a competitive commercial television field depends on an overwhelming emphasis on entertainment. Any other course leads to financial disaster.

But in the United Kingdom we do not have a competitive commercial situation, and I hope we never shall. We have an element of competition to be sure, but it is not commercial competition, and the balance of programmes on the BBC's side is not affected by it at all. From the start it was clear that ITA's programme policy would be to undercut the BBC. The BBC was in the field; it had the whole audience then available, and left to itself, it would in a few years have got the whole population of the United Kingdom as its audience. ITA's initial task was to wean away from the BBC as much of the existing audience as possible and to court the allegiance of the newcomers.

The general balance of BBC programmes was unaffected, and during the competitive era the BBC's proportion of serious programmes in main viewing hours actually went up—not down as was forecast by the gloomy exponents of Gresham's Law, but had the BBC been in full commercial competition, Gresham's Law would have operated and the proportion would most certainly have gone down.

Television has many competitive weapons, most of them minor tactical weapons which the BBC uses. The one big strategic weapon, the hydrogen bomb of television competition, is to lower the proportion of intelligent programmes in main viewing hours to below the level of one's competitor. This is the most effective weapon of all, and it is the one the BBC has resolutely refused to employ in spite of the fact that it has consistently been used against it by the ITA.

I do not think that a full statement of the BBC's attitude to the competitive situation was made until my speech to the Radio Industries Club in September, 1957. I quote the relevant passages from it:

Commercial television 'is a branch—and a very important branch—of the sales side of British industry. It must earn its living by attracting and keeping a steady, flat rate, predictable audience, and by selling that audience in advance to advertising clients. It has to attract its audience and then keep it up to specification. That is the great problem for them. They cannot afford to sell their audience in short measure to advertising clients. Their task is to present a programme to the public which will secure a steady predictable audience—an audience which a client can buy in advance with confidence. That is the business of commercial television. They must stick to it or fail. Being good business men they will stick to it. What is the technique? Well, of course, they know more about it than I do. But I would expect them increasingly to go for well-tried formulae—things which either the BBC or they or the Americans have devised and built up as popular favourites with big followings. I think it will be very difficult for them to be anything but slightly old-fashioned. I know a few very modern-minded men in commercial television who I am sure would wish it to be otherwise, but I fear that the compulsion of the predictable audience will in the end force them into this pattern. However, ITA will undoubtedly give pleasure to a very large number of viewers. It will be a faithful servant of industry, and I should not be surprised if it makes a lot of money for its shareholders. But it would be a mistake to expect it to be a reflection of the advancing tastes and aspirations or of the perplexities of an educated democracy in the making. Such a policy would make for unpredictable audiences and it would almost certainly lower the average audience. In short, I suspect it would be bad business for commercial television.

'Now the BBC is on a completely different course . . . simply because it has an entirely different way of earning its living. To the BBC the average audience is of no real importance except in so far as people on whom the BBC depends may attach importance to it . . . The BBC does not have to sell its average audience to anyone. So it is free to concentrate on audiences in the plural—audiences for individual programmes. And we measure our successes and our failures to a large extent by whether or not we achieve the appropriate audience for each programme. Our audiences are not steady. They are variable. Some are quite astonishingly greater than we at first expected, some the other way round. The reason for this is the BBC's policy, which it is possible for us to carry out because we earn our living by direct payments from our customers with no intermediaries whose business interests have to be served. What is the BBC's policy? It has on occasions been stated as keeping slightly ahead of what is commonly supposed to be public taste. Now that policy has sometimes been misinterpreted by ill-disposed persons as a desire to improve the human race—a sort of superior condescending attitude—almost a "holier than thou" approach. But this is nonsense . . . Just about the time the BBC was formed, this country was embarking upon a big expansion of State secondary education, which has been going on ever since. Before then only a small proportion of our people had any secondary education at all. Now the proportion is much

MONOPOLY AND COMPETITION

greater. What is more: an enormous number of children are now brought up by parents who themselves have had secondary education. You see it is having a kind of snowball effect. It is going on so rapidly that "what is commonly supposed" is always a bit out of date. I've already told you that "slightly old-fashioned" is what you have got to be if you are to ensure a predictable audience. But if you go up nearer to the forefront of taste and intellectual interest—as the BBC will—you are in some pretty unpredictable country. You never quite know what is going to happen next. But nevertheless it's a very important thing to do. If we regard television as the main instrument of communication in the future—and I do so regard it—we must see to it that at least one of our national channels is modern, up-to-date and devoted to satisfying the requirements of an educated democracy in the making. That is the course which the BBC television service will follow . . .

'. . . You can't expect a commercial system aiming at a large predictable audience not to get it in time. This is especially true when the national network (the BBC) is aiming at something quite different and is not, in fact, competing with them in those terms at all. If and when commercial television achieves an average of more than half the total audience . . . it will not surprise the BBC or deflect it from its course in any way.'

Two and a half years later I delivered an address in New York and again made public reference to the BBC's attitude to its competitive position. I said:

'About half the BBC's prime viewing time is devoted to programmes of information, of ideas and of important works of art. The competing advertising network does not altogether neglect these things, but it devotes a much smaller proportion of its prime time to them. Therefore if you take as a self-evident truth the proposition that entertainment is always more popular than thought or cultivated taste, you will assume that the BBC is deliberately making a present of the mass audience to its competitor. The BBC would be prepared to let its average audience go down to one-third, maybe even one-quarter, of the total rather than lower its professional standards or reduce its high proportion of intelligent programmes.' I was able to add, 'But in fact this has not happened.'

TELEVISION: A CRITICAL REVIEW

These public statements, and others like them, were well received in both camps. The protagonists of public service television took them as indications that the BBC was remaining true to form. The protagonists of commercial television were reassured because they took them to indicate that the BBC would not use its full competitive strength.

Nevertheless the ITA's competition for the audience raised in our minds the whole question of the BBC's future and indeed its very survival. I said in my New York speech that we would be prepared to allow our proportion of the audience to go down to one-third, even perhaps one-quarter, of the total rather than reduce the quantity of our thoughtful programmes in main viewing hours, but I was always very conscious of the danger of letting that proportion slip too far. How far dare we let it go? I personally was confident of our being able to justify the continued existence of BBC television if our proportion did not go below a third, so long as we could demonstrate our ability to get two-thirds whenever we wanted to. If it went to a quarter I should have been a good deal less confident but not in despair; below a quarter would have been very dangerous. It would have been hard to justify the continued existence of an expensive and comprehensive public service covering a very wide range of human interest including entertainment, if only a small minority of the people were using it, and the fact that the BBC's revenue came to it through the agency of a government department would have made the situation doubly difficult.

But worst of all the quality of the BBC's programmes would have suffered in spite of the stability of its revenue. Artists and other kinds of performer do not broadcast for money alone, especially the best ones, nor do the best staff producers remain however much they are paid unless they have an audience; politicians, statesmen and people with messages want the big audience, not small minorities. A television network is a massive medium of communication, which means that it must have a massive audience to communicate with. If the BBC's audience in those first few years had dropped below the danger point, whatever that may have been, the best people, however much they may have disliked commercial television, would have gone over to it no matter what money was offered by the BBC to retain them, because the audience would have been essential to them.

Suppose the BBC had competed wholeheartedly with ITA. It had most of the trump cards, experience, know-how, technical resources—everything except novelty and advertisements. It would not have been at all difficult for the BBC to have put ITA out of business, indeed to have prevented it ever properly getting into business, during the first two years. If the BBC had decided to use the big weapon, it would have concentrated on entertainment between 7.0 and 10.30 p.m., putting all thoughtful material before or after this period, and much reducing its total quantity. It would have paid anything to retain the services of skilled staff so as to delay ITA getting the know-how. ITA would have been strangled at birth; the millions of pounds, which were nearly lost as it was, would indeed have been lost, and the cry would have gone up to the government to rescue their child from the jaws of the monster.

During that critical period the BBC made no demonstration of its full competitive strength, and it was right, because by doing so it would have created a 'vast wasteland', which would have been impossible to recover afterwards. Nobody would have had any good out of it, least of all the British people; ITA would have been eliminated and the BBC would have lost its integrity. One of the basic calculations of the investors in commercial television was that the BBC would not use the big weapon, because if it did it would destroy itself. So the BBC in 1955 appeared to most of its own members to be in an impossible position; if it did not compete it was lost because it would have no audience, and if it did compete it would win a Pyrrhic victory and become something not worth preserving.

ITA pressure on the BBC began with the enticement of technical and professional staff—the men with the know-how. Some of them were offered more responsible positions than they had with the BBC; all were offered greatly increased salaries, and about four hundred found the temptation impossible to resist. The fact that in many cases the advantages were only temporary made little difference to young men with wives and families to keep and educate. Likewise the impoverishment of the BBC staff was only temporary because we had so many good men and women coming up, but the onslaught had a disturbing effect on the staff who remained. Morale went down. Many newspapers, especially those financially involved in commercial television, did their best to exacerbate the situation by hammering the BBC and trying to represent it as an effete organization which would collapse at the first breath of competition from big business, and Norman Collins publicly said that BBC television would soon grind to a halt. This sort of rubbish had little effect on some of us but it did have a powerful effect on many of the younger professionals who were concerned about their futures. They did not want to leave the BBC but they needed an employer with an assured future; if the BBC ship was sinking, they would have to board another.

I took over in 1956 from a régime which I always think of as the Barnes-McGivern régime; Sir George Barnes, the Director and Cecil McGivern, the Controller of Programmes, had been the guiding figures in a period of great expansion, leaders in building up BBC television from a relatively small affair into a large well administered service with steadily rising professional standards. Barnes left to become Vice-Chancellor of the University of North Staffordshire; McGivern, before my appointment, was promoted and later left to join Granada TV. I was allowed to appoint a Controller of Programmes from outside the BBC, Kenneth Adam, who at the time was General Manager of the Hulton Press, but who had previously had a great deal of experience in the BBC including the Controllership of the Light Programme in Sir William Haley's time. I think of the next period as the Beadle-Adam régime, which lasted until midsummer, 1961, when I retired, and Kenneth Adam succeeded me.

It was under the Beadle-Adam régime that commercial competition was met and, I believe, mastered. This may seem a big claim to make, but I believe it to be broadly true. I found in Adam a man who shared with me a considerable zest for a fight, and a philosophy which was not shared with all our colleagues.

Our thinking went as follows. The majority of the British people are not morons; they may be under-educated; their intellectual interests may be narrow; their innate capacity for artistic appreciation may be under-developed. This backwardness, which is real, up to a point, is not nearly so great as is commonly supposed in cheap journalistic and commercial television circles. The strong belief which Adam and I shared was that, given a choice between a television service with a high proportion of intelligent material and one with a low proportion, the majority of viewers would go for the latter at first and gradually but surely come to prefer the former. The process would be very gradual, hence the need for inexhaustible patience.

In this belief we parted company with those who had always claimed Gresham's Law as inevitably applicable to television. The so-called law asserts that bad coinage always drives out good coinage, which is probably true, but it does not follow that in all circumstances bad television drives out good. In a situation of unbridled commercial television competition Gresham's Law does apply; you can see it happening in America, and it would happen here, if we had two or more competing commercial networks. But if the only element of competition is between one commercial network and one network which does not depend on advertiser's money, and therefore does not have to lower its standards, it is not inconceivable that the good might eventually drive out the bad.

To translate this rather theoretical approach into practical terms: We expected that our initial refusal to compete with ITA on its own terms would result *at first* in ITA's attracting a heavy majority of the viewers who were in a position to choose, but we expected that ITA's big lead would gradually be reduced. The swing (which of course would be subject to many ups and downs) would be a slow one covering many years, but in the end would result in an overall lead for the BBC. At or before that point ITA would come out and compete with us on our terms, which would mean increasing their own proportion of intelligent programmes between 7.0 and 10.30 p.m. and so raising their standards nearer to our level.

Most of my senior colleagues in the BBC have regarded this thinking as unreal or too optimistic, and I can't claim that we have yet entirely proved it otherwise. For instance, my Director General, Sir Ian Jacob, often said to me that if ever the BBC's average audience were to get anywhere near ITA's, he would begin to think there was something wrong with BBC television.

In 1956 only a small minority of viewers could receive ITA,

and for most people it was a choice of BBC or nothing, but the viewing habits of the small minority which could choose between BBC and ITA were regarded as indicative of the tastes of the whole nation. Immense publicity was given to the fact that about seventy per cent of viewing by the minority was to ITA, and the BBC with a mere thirty per cent was judged to be on the way out. Advertisers and commercial television people here and in America were impressed, and the death knell of public service broadcasting was being sounded. Since then many changes have come about, and now that nearly everybody in Britain can receive either network at will, about fifty per cent are viewing BBC. The death knell has become inaudible. Six years ago ITA was disassociating itself as much as possible from the BBC and proclaiming itself as 'The True Voice of the People' and the BBC as out of touch, but now ITA is claiming to be very like the BBC. I hope this is wishful thinking and not mere Pilkington propaganda, because if it is wishful thinking, it indicates a desire to be more like the BBC, and it could lead to a better proportion of intelligent programmes in British commercial television. It suggests that the ITA has learned from recent BBC audience ratings that a well-balanced service can *in the long run*, be good business. Having learned the lesson, ITA may well start competing with the BBC on the BBC's own terms, and this will be Gresham's Law in reverse. If and when this happens the BBC will have won the only television competition worth winning.

The only real disaster, that could overtake British television now, would be a second commercial network competing with the existing one. Neither could afford to take the long view, and each would have to use the ultimate weapon against the other. We should have the bloody battle of the ratings with no holds barred. Advertising revenue, commercial television's life blood, would be directly related to the respective ratings of the competitors. Low ratings, even for short periods, would mean financial loss, and balanced programming would become bad business.

I have said elsewhere that the exclusion of the advertising sponsor from British commercial television has had a beneficial influence on programme standards, but here I must add that the absence of competition in the commercial field is a factor of at least equal importance.

CHAPTER 8

Television and Advertising

TELEVISION is an industry in its own right, and to treat it otherwise is to mistreat it. To set up a television station or network as an instrument for the sale of goods, with some entertainment thrown in as bait, is to treat television as something much less than an industry in its own right. I know of no other industry which has been treated so badly in this respect; its potentialities are inhibited, and its status is deplorably low in countries where this has happened. Our British record is a poor one but I think we have avoided the worst excesses. The motives behind the introduction of commercial television in this country were parasitical, the principal driving force behind the pressure group being the desire to climb on the back of the television industry by taking advantage of its inherent financial weakness. They wanted to tame it and make use of it for purposes which had nothing but bondage to offer to television; nothing except money. The British people had for decades grown accustomed to paying for their broadcasting through the licence, and there was absolutely no reason to suppose they would not pay in the same way for a second television network. The Government at that time was drawing enormous profits out of the BBC, and there would have been no difficulty in financing another television network by the traditional British method; indeed the financial condition of British television was so good that advertising revenue was wholly unnecessary to its fullest development. The painful story of how British television came to be enmeshed is told by Professor H. H. Wilson in *Pressure Group* published in 1961 by Secker and Warburg. It is the story of a malaise which may attack a democracy when it gets slack, and results in the will of a few busy persons prevailing over the will of the majority.

TELEVISION: A CRITICAL REVIEW

On the credit side it must be recorded that many members of the Tory Party and of the Government itself shared with the Labour Party a genuine fear that it would mean the loss of one of the two basic freedoms of television, and a consequent debasement of standards. While the Tory whips were put on to drive the measure through Parliament, the opposition was so strong, even amongst many of those who were compelled to support it, that great care was taken in the Act to provide safeguards against the worst excesses of unbridled commercialism. Especially important was the clause prohibiting sponsorship. Looking at British commercial television from the outside, I am inclined to think that the Act made the best of a bad job, and that ours is the best of the wholly commercial television services in the world.

Professor Wilson's book is the political side of the story, but there is another side; there was an unusually strong demand from large sections of British industry in the early nineteen fifties for more opportunities for advertising their goods. Wartime restrictions especially on paper had only recently been lifted, and a real boom in consumer goods was developing, but industry felt that there were insufficient opportunities for telling the public about the large range of new goods which were becoming available. Television was obviously an excellent medium for this, and industry was not averse to harnessing the television horse to the industrial chariot.

Advertising is an essential function in a modern industrial society, because the modern western way of life depends on producing vastly more types and quantities of goods than are strictly speaking necessary. The basic necessities of life need no advertising, but the frills, the extra amenities do. They can soon become conventional necessities, and people can be nearly as miserable without them as they would be without food, but they must be told about them; they won't even ask for them, let alone miss them, unless they know they are there. Advertising does this for them, and by stimulating demand it keeps the wheels of industry going and keeps people in employment. This cycle of production, distribution and consumption of goods which are not basic necessities of life, is the machinery of a high material standard of living, and advertising plays an essential part in it; so anybody who objects to advertising *per se* is

TELEVISION AND ADVERTISING

taking a wholly unrealistic view of our present situation. We all depend on it directly or indirectly. The problem of advertising is that it has practically no medium of its own; so it sticks itself on to other things and all too often defaces them. Our newspapers, other things being equal, would be better without advertisements; our buses and tube stations would be less ugly; our cities and main roads would be more beautiful. I can think of few things in life that would not be improved in appearance or efficiency or both by the removal of the advertisements which now stick to them, but I must confess that I see no way of avoiding this state of affairs. It could be better regulated perhaps; the worst excesses could be mitigated, but the phenomenon must remain with us, and it is essentially a parasitic phenomenon.

Mass advertising has produced in its hosts a state of financial dependence. Their prices to their own customers have become adjusted to the sums they receive from their advertising parasites, and this is particularly true of newspapers whose prices are ludicrously low in relation to the services they render, but everybody has got so used to paying these low prices that they would think they were being robbed, if they were asked to pay the true price for a newspaper. So the host and the parasite have become partners, neither capable of survival without the other.

Whether this, on balance, is a good or a bad thing cannot be settled in general terms. The newspapers have obviously judged that it is a good thing for them and they are probably right. Most churches are short of money and would make good advertising media, but no doubt they judge that on balance advertising detergents from the pulpit would not be a good thing, and I am sure they are right too. When we come to the use of television as an advertising medium we find a very sharp division of opinion as to whether it is good or bad; I think it is very bad for television.

I would like to see a really competent appraisal of the country's advertising needs. I do not know what they are, and I doubt whether anybody else knows. If we had too little advertising the economy would begin to run down; if we had too much, we should be wasting our money, and defacing our surroundings unnecessarily. It is something which needs much more thought and planning on a national scale than, so far as

I am aware, it has ever had before.

A great deal of our present-day advertising seems to have the aim of increasing the sales of particular products at the expense of others of the same type often made by the same firm. Whether this increases the total volume of trade or tends towards a better quality of goods I do not know, but if it does neither, it is wasteful from the point of view of the economy and irksome to the public. Unquestionably we have got to provide media for the advertising of consumer goods up to the point of maximum expansion of the economy, but it seems to me to be very important that we should not carry it much beyond this point. Every host on which the advertiser settles is damaged or weakened by it in some degree. Some are damaged more than others and it is important to keep this damage to the minimum compatible with the fullest possible expansion of manufacture and consumption. I don't suppose it is possible to be absolutely precise in this matter, but I do think that more information is required.

The case for commercial broadcasting usually rests less on the needs of the economy than on the claim that advertising pays not only for itself but for the broadcasting service too, so the people don't have to pay. The fact of course is that the people pay for it anyway, but the only other method of getting the money out of them—the licence system—is difficult, perhaps even impossible, to administer in underdeveloped countries, and I so am inclined to think that the case for the commercial approach in such countries is well nigh unanswerable. But in wealthy countries like Britain, France, and West Germany, very populous, with small compact territories and highly-evolved administrations, the licence system has proved eminently workable and successful. It presents no major problems provided the danger of political control is avoided as it has been in Britain. On financial grounds there is not, and never has been, a valid case for commercial broadcasting in Britain. The only valid argument for commercial broadcasting here would be one based on the needs of our country's economy; if it could be shown that without it our material standard of living would suffer, exports would suffer and unemployment would result; if all this could be supported with reliable data, then the case for commercial broadcasting in Britain would merit consideration, but no such case has ever been made.

In the absence of any such case one must look at the other side of the picture and enquire what damage, if any, is suffered by broadcasting when for financial reasons it enters into a host/parasite relationship with advertising. I will deal with this point from a general not a specifically British angle.

1. Broadcast advertising is in the quite literal sense an impertinence, seldom bearing any relationship to the programme it interrupts; it demands a mental switch, which to attentive people is an irksome strain. Vast numbers of people adapt themselves to it quite happily, but only by allowing themselves to become relatively inattentive and under-concentrated. If they don't develop scatty minds, their enjoyment is much reduced, but unfortunately many of them do. This applies mainly to advertisements of the interruptive kind, not so much to advertisements in the intervals between programmes.

2. Interruptive advertising, when it interrupts programmes of information gets between the viewer and the information, and this is particularly bad in the United States. Four nights running at around six in the evening I viewed the national and local news bulletins from one Chicago station, an affiliate of one of the networks. I found the national and international news almost impossible to follow because it was so heavily larded with irrelevant information about cigarettes, soap flakes, shoes and so on, all treated by the news reader as if they were as important as the news itself. When there was a long item of news, the item itself was cut in two to make way for a commercial, and I reached the end of the bulletin little wiser about what was going on in the world. If the Americans want an informed public opinion I think they will have to do something about this. Advertising is setting up an almost impenetrable barrier between the viewer and the information. The local Chicago news was much better, because local advertisements were not so plentiful, and the barrier was much easier to penetrate.

3. Advertising under the 'Sponsorship' system (the American system) leads to immense quantities of mostly very poor programmes and to very bad programme balance. Mr Newton Minow's 'Vast Wasteland'.

4. Advertising under the British system leads to bad programme balance in main viewing hours but not necessarily to

bad programmes.

5. Advertising involves advance contracts with advertisers, which in turn inhibit flexibility. There is no doubt that the advertising straightjacket discourages by financial penalties what is perhaps the most important of television's functions—the live reporting of events as they are taking place.

6. The straightjacket will probably make international live television much more restricted than it ought to be. I deal with this more fully in another chapter.

I believe that television and radio are defaced by advertising more than any other medium is defaced by it, and this is my reason for thinking that any country sufficiently wealthy and well administered to operate the licence system successfully should stick to it, unless it can be shown indisputably that the economy of the country will suffer serious danger if it is not supported by television advertising.

There are two distinct kinds of advertisement. The informative kind and the persuasive kind. Commercial television lives on the latter, but it is interesting to note that the BBC has quite recently entered the field of informative advertising, and at the time of writing this chapter the BBC has broadcast two programmes under the title 'Choice'. It has begun as a monthly programme, and I hope it will be much more frequent when its technique and machinery have been developed rather further. It has already achieved an audience of getting on for five million viewers, and it could have an extremely valuable effect on the country's economy, because it seeks to show viewers the qualities to be favoured and the qualities to be avoided when choosing goods. If it succeeds in its objective it will tend to encourage the good manufacturer and discourage the shoddy one in the British home market. This in turn will raise the prestige of British goods everywhere and will help the export trade far more effectively than any amount of persuasive advertising. Although it is not one of the declared objectives of 'Choice' to advertise goods in the ordinary sense, nevertheless the programme cannot fail to be a strong vehicle of important information, bringing to the attention of millions of viewers the available products of British industry, products of which they would not otherwise know the existence. It seems to me that this is one of the more important services which television

TELEVISION AND ADVERTISING

can render to the industrial and commercial health of the country, and I hope the BBC will keep it up.

When the British television industry was compelled in 1954 to advertise persuasively the products of other industries there were some curious consequences. Before the new network came on the air I asked a number of senior industrialists whether they were going to use television to advertise their products, and those I spoke to said they were going to use it. They did not seem very happy or enthusiastic about it, but they gave the impression that they felt they ought to support the Tories in this matter, but the chief reason seemed to be fear lest competitors would get in ahead of them and derive substantial advantage thereby. I got the impression, which has been much strengthened since, that as soon as a new medium is created potential advertisers will go into it, not to improve their own positions so much as to avoid slipping back; the medium is there and if one does not use it another will and so gain an advantage. Whether industry as a whole gains an overall advantage I rather doubt. It seems that persuasive television advertising is more an instrument of protection for firms or groups of firms against the risk of having the bread taken out of their mouths by rivals, but it is an inflationary form of protection, for which in the end the customer has to pay in the price of the goods he buys. If the public were withholding their purchasing power—in other words saving their money—on a nationally undesirable scale, there would be a case for propaganda to persuade them to disgorge more of it on consumer goods. But is this so?

Soon there were signs of dissatisfaction with the ITA, a state owned monopoly which had granted monopolistic franchises to its fourteen contracting programme companies, not one of them in competition with anybody else in its own field, and raising their rates whenever it suited them. This led to a movement to break the monopoly; and I have on many occasions been approached by business men and by politicians to support a move to get the BBC to apply to the Postmaster General for permission to accept paid advertising in its television service, permission which would probably have been forthcoming. The drive behind the movement is the desire to break the ITA's commercial monopoly by putting the BBC into competition with it and so to bring down the advertising rates. I need hardly add that the BBC would have nothing to do with it. It is somewhat ironical that the BBC's monopoly in its own field was widely criticized ten years ago and was held to be a major reason for creating the ITA. A few years later it was being suggested unofficially but energetically that the BBC should lend itself to assist the breakup of the ITA monopoly.

Another alternative now being canvassed is the creation of yet another commercial television network, presumably under quite separate management, to compete for advertising business with the existing one. From the purely business point of view I can see enormous disadvantages in this course. The amount of audience exposure to advertisements will always be about the same whether we have one or two or twenty commercial television networks, and it is difficult to see who is going to get anything out of it, except of course those who make programmes and 'Commercials', and television transmitting gear.

A real danger would be to the standard of programmes. The present relatively high standard of British commercial television is in large measure due to the pace set by the BBC. During the 'Pilkington period' commercial television has tried to claim that its service of programmes is like that of the BBC, but in fact it is very different. However, there is quite an urge to appear to be keeping up with the BBC which is all to the good, but a second commercial network would undo all this. The two networks would be locked in mortal combat with each other; the battle of the ratings would be on in a big way, and the BBC would cease to influence commercial television standards.

The ITA and its programme contractors have on the whole made the best of a bad job. The people operating the network, for the most part did not advocate commercial television in the first place; they took it on after the Government had imposed it on the country as a *fait accomplit*. It is exceedingly difficult under an advertising system of finance to maintain a well-balanced service of programmes in the public interest, but they have gone some way towards it, and it is not enough to explain it as entirely due to BBC pace-making. There are men in commercial television who regard it as something more than a licence to print money, and who regard intelligent programming as something more than a device to impress 'The Establishment'; but the system is working against them.

TELEVISION AND ADVERTISING

Meanwhile the future relations between television and industry need a lot more study. Already a vast torrent of persuasive advertising goes out on one network and a slender trickle of consumer information on the other. The public do not get much real help from ITA's glossy pictures of goods being consumed often in idyllic circumstances, the exaggerated claims and meaningless statements which too often accompany them, and the jingles which give an impression of spuriousness to that type of advertising. Better education and growing sophistication will bring with them a demand for more information such as the better type of magazine advertising provides. Above all the public needs more objective surveys of the comparative advantages and disadvantages of various makes of goods. We may be some distance from a popular revulsion against the kind of advertising which nags without informing, but I think it will come.

There never was a time when communication between industry and its customers was so necessary as it is today. Most buying is done in large impersonal stores and supermarkets, where the staff often know no more about the goods they are selling than the customers do. The range and complexity of the goods on offer is prodigious; the customer is bewildered and too often there is no one to help. It is not only a question of getting good value for money, it is also a question of knowing what particular article is the best for the purpose in mind, and indeed whether such an article exists. The specialized expert retailer is on the decline, and we need something to take his place. Informative advertising is the answer, probably the only answer, but television is not being used to the best advantage so long as most of its advertising combines a maximum of shouting with a minimum of information. People are not helped by this sort of thing, indeed they are being fooled by it and they are beginning to know it. The truth is that too many industrialists are not much concerned with imparting to customers the information they need; they are much more concerned with trying to persuade people that one brand is better than others of its kind, and they are all trying to do it at once, the result being a confusing cacophony of half-baked claims and counter-claims spiced up with appeals to cupidity, snobbery and sex.

But I think we must assume, however regrettable it may be

to some of us, that persuasive advertising is something that television will have to carry for many years to come. For a lot of complex reasons the United States could not have avoided it; it has crept into Canada, Australia and more recently into New Zealand. Europe, to its credit, has largely avoided it so far, though Britain by some curious aberration let it in, almost as it were, by mistake. The underdeveloped countries will be hard put to it to maintain television in any other way. I see no point now in merely deploring the invasion of the advertiser; his foot is very firmly in the television door and we are not likely to get it out in measurable time.

The problem is to devise some system by which the advertiser's influence on television programmes is reduced to a minimum. There are three advertising systems in the world today. We have much experience of the first two and hardly any of the third. They are:

1. The Sponsorship System.
    In America this system has proved very unsatisfactory. It should be avoided at all costs.

2. The Differential Rate Spot Advertising System.
    This is the British system. It is much better, but it leads to an over-emphasis on entertainment at times when large audiences are available.

3. The Flat Rate Rotatory System.
    I know of only one country, New Zealand, where this is used. It is probably too early to make a full assessment of it. It is described on the next page.

I am a professional broadcaster and naturally look upon the whole business of broadcast advertising with regret, so I think it better to expose it through the mind of someone in the advertising business, who makes a large part of his living from broadcast advertising. He is not likely to share my particular form of subjectivity. I quote Mr Fairfax Cone, Chairman of the Executive Committee of Foote, Cone and Belding, one of America's leading advertising firms. In a talk to the Broadcasting Advertising Club of Chicago on October 10, 1961, he said:

TELEVISION AND ADVERTISING

'American business became enamoured of show business way back in the heyday of radio. The devotion reached the stage of red hot passion with television. But I think that disillusion has set in. If it has, as I think it has, and most advertisers simply view television as another, even though greater, medium of communication that they are willing to leave the communicators to operate, we can have fair sailing, together with all manner of just and pleasant rewards.'

This is a remarkable statement. It seems to be a plea for the death of sponsorship, and a recognition that broadcasting is the proper job of the broadcasters ('the Communicators').

In the same speech Mr Cone suggested an alternative to the Sponsorship System. He put it forward in two parts:

1. 'To balance the weekly fare between regular and special entertainment features and special features in the fields of controversy and ideas—even in the arts.'

This is what the BBC would call 'Balanced Programming.'

2. '... the second step in this plan is to revolve advertisers through the total weeks' programming; to cut out, as it were, preferred positions in the weekly schedule, and to open this up to experimentation, with every advertiser paying his share. The method is as simple as the rotation of commercials by a single advertiser for six products through two weekly shows; only the networks would rotate *all* advertisers through *all* except special shows. There are people who oppose this. But I believe they are short-sighted. Because, if they hold to their preferred positions in certain large-audience programmes, their competitors must seek to equal them (they have no choice) and the level of television programming will remain precisely what it is—which is a national disgrace.'

Here is Mr Cone advocating what I have called the 'Flat Rate Rotatory System'. So far as I know nobody has practical experience of this system except New Zealand, and that only very recently. In theory it is much more promising than the Sponsorship System, and we have this prominent and experienced American advertising practitioner advocating it and condemning sponsorship. It could have important advantages over our

British system too, perhaps freeing ITA from the compulsion to overload with entertainment the main evening periods, for which the advertisers pay specially high rates, because all advertisers would pay the same rates after about six o'clock, and they would take turns for the more desirable spots. Thus ITA might achieve the one really important liberty it now lacks—the liberty to broadcast a well-balanced evening programme.

Whatever may be the future of British television, it would be foolish to ignore advertising as a more or less permanent feature of it. The task of future statesmen will be to keep advertising in its proper place and to prevent it from curbing the liberty of the broadcasters to fulfil their role which is to serve the public interest.

CHAPTER 9

Education and Instruction

Two very useful expressions are gaining currency in America, 'Educational Television' (ETV) and 'Instructional Television' (ITV). I am trying to avoid the use in this book of the expression Independent Television (ITV) to describe British commercial television. It is not the proper name, and I want to reserve the initials ITV for 'Instructional Television'.

Most people would agree that education is a good thing, but it is a rather vague concept, and when people talk of education in broadcasting one is often left wondering what exactly they are talking about. So I had better try and define what I mean by it here. Educational broadcasting to me means broadcasting which is informative or which stimulates thought or which develops latent tastes for good art of all kinds; it is the kind of broadcasting which broadens people's mental horizons, encourages a proper sense of values and enhances wisdom. It is a positive approach to people as distinct from pure entertainment which aims to amuse and relax without making demands on their minds. But there is no reason in the world why educational broadcasting should not at the same time be entertaining; indeed it is usually far more effective if it amuses and interests simultaneously. To engage a man's emotions and his intellect together is to treat him as a whole person, which is how we all like to be treated.

I was asked at a recent international conference in Washington, whether in Britain we clearly mark our educational programmes so that the viewer can know in advance whether he is to be educated or entertained. I replied that for my own private information as Director I used to keep some sort of a score of these things, but so far as the public was concerned, the more confusion we could create the better. To some extent this also applies to producers. A good producer of educational programmes (as opposed to instructional programmes), must in communicating his material attract and hold the attention of his audience. No matter how profound his material may be, he is unsuccessful if he bores the viewer or fails to treat him as a whole person. For this reason it is a tremendous advantage within a broadcasting organization to mix up your producing staff as much as possible. The influence of the pure show business man on the educator is very important and influence in the other direction is equally important. I have always put great value on staff clubs, restaurants and other facilities for mixing together men and women working in different departments; the educators become less ponderous, the show business types less brash. The education, or training of a broadcasting staff is of immense importance to the quality of their work, and the most potent element in their training is the influence they have on each other.

This is one of the many reasons why I have no sympathy whatsoever with any proposal to set up an educational network in Britain. Even if that network were controlled by the BBC, still more if it were not, it would be dominated by professional educators trained in the technique of imparting knowledge to captive audiences. These good people would be divorced from the stimulating influence of men and women who have lived their lives attracting and holding the attention of non-captive audiences—audiences free to turn the knob if they are bored as most of them would be.

Much of the impetus behind the demand for an educational network comes from commercial television, and it is not difficult to understand their interest in it. With the probability of only four nationwide television networks for the next ten or fifteen years, the pressure group claims two for commercial and is trying to prevent the BBC from having more than one. An educational network would sterilize the remaining channel and thus leave the BBC with only one. So competitive commercial television would become the dominant factor in British television, and the 'wasteland' would come in under the guise of education.

But apart from the commercial interests, there have from time to time been suggestions from more serious people that we

EDUCATION AND INSTRUCTION

should have one educational network in Britain. I have never seen a carefully worked out statement of what is meant by an educational network, but I imagine it would confine itself to material commonly regarded as having cultural value, leaving sport, light entertainment and probably news to the other channels. In addition to the impoverishment which would result from lack of contact with the world of entertainment, the absence of entertainment from the programmes would guarantee a minute audience. To run any kind of a network with high-quality material, whether it be educational or not, is an immensely expensive thing to do. The BBC's present network has involved enormous capital expenditure, and the annual costs are of the order of twenty-five million pounds now. An educational network would be no cheaper except in so far as its hours might be shorter. The BBC's Third Programme in sound is defensible on the grounds that sound channels are relatively plentiful and sound costs relatively low, but a repetition in television would be a wasteful extravagance.

America has about sixty educational television stations. I have visited some of them and taken part in their programmes as a speaker. They have a well-deserved prestige in their own country, not because of their inherent merit, but because they are inevitably compared with competitive commercial. But it is television on a shoe-string, starved for money, understaffed and with very small audiences. In America educational television is a protest against the debasement of the rest of their television. No such protest is needed here.

I have met senior members of American commercial networks who would welcome a well-financed national educational network, and one day I asked one of them to enlarge upon it. As a citizen he thought it would be a good thing; as a commercial broadcaster he wanted to be free from the nagging of the Federal Communications Commission and the more intelligent elements in American society. In short he wanted to be left alone to get on with his job of selling goods to the American people, and if only some other organization could take over the job of doing the non-commercial stuff, it would make life so much easier for him. This attitude seems to be repeating itself here (vide the ITA's proposal for an educational network and a second commercial network). But it won't work in either country because in broadcasting entertainment is the indispensable ally of education.

And yet ETV is something we want more of in this country. The BBC's single network provides about as much as any single network can; the ITA does not, but might be induced to do more if the BBC can show that audience ratings need not suffer by it. We must avoid the error of imagining that the *broadcasting* of more ETV is the object of the exercise. The object is to have more ETV actually received on the screens in people's homes. A special ETV network would greatly increase the total volume of ETV being blown out into the ether, but it could, by drawing it away from the existing high audience networks, result in less ETV being received at the viewing end. It could therefore be an educationally retrograde step, and a very costly one into the bargain. The only sure way of substantially increasing the volume of ETV on the home screen (apart from inducing ITA to do more at peak viewing hours), is to have another public service network fully co-ordinated with the existing one. This in effect means another BBC network, and it is exactly what the BBC have always wanted from the start.

The BBC has always contended that it cannot completely fulfil the obligations placed upon it by its Charter, unless it has two complementary television networks, and though the terms of the charter are a little vague in these matters, I believe the BBC's contention to be a sound one. But the more important question is the use to which the two complementary networks would be put, and the benefits which would accrue to the public from having a double rather than a single public service. In my opinion the benefits would be very great indeed and most of them would fall within the sphere of ETV as broadly defined by me. Both BBC networks would offer comprehensive services; each would be 'balanced' like the present single one, containing a mixture of interest and entertainment. Anyone staying with one of the networks (and many people are surprisingly lazy with the switch) would in the course of an evening receive a very wide range of material, as he does now, but the other network would have been planned in such a way that, if a programme comes up which is not to his taste, the viewer will be able to switch over to the other BBC network and be sure of finding there a programme of a different character. I have

EDUCATION AND INSTRUCTION

already pointed out that the BBC's present network has about one-third ETV in peak hours exclusive of drama. If drama of real cultural value were included in the count, the proportion would be more like one-half. Two complementary networks both with this proportion of ETV and planned so that when one was showing ETV the other was showing entertainment, would result in a fairly continuous supply of ETV available on one network or the other. An educational television network would produce no more ETV than this, but infinitely less of it would reach the people.

The preamble to the current Royal Charter of the BBC, after referring to the number of receiving licences taken out by the people, goes on to say this:

'Whereas in view of the widespread interest which is thereby and by other evidences shown to be taken by Our Peoples in the broadcasting services and of the great value of such services as means of disseminating information, education and entertainment, We believe . . .'

So education is recognized as one of the major functions of the BBC in which there is evidence of widespread *interest*, but the Charter makes no attempt to define education, nor to say in what proportion it should be provided in relation to the other two ingredients. All that is very wisely left to the BBC. I think the word 'interest' is important. I have often thought that a better exposition of the BBC's role would be to make provision for the education of the people by interesting and entertaining them. I do not suppose that any but a very small number of people would ever dream of turning to television with the conscious object of being educated, but they do want to be interested. The dividing line between being interested and being entertained is often a very difficult one to draw, and it is much better that it should be so.

An educational network would have to eschew popular entertainment. Its service of information, whatever that might be, would almost certainly lack the support of a world-wide news coverage. It would presumably not maintain fleets of mobile camera units for the live reporting of political, sporting and other events. It would be a network lacking most of the essential ingredients of 'interest'. In short it would not have an audience, and without an audience it would not educate. If however it were decided to provide the new network with all the essential ingredients of 'interest' and call it educational, we should find ourselves with another network barely distinguishable in its policy from the BBC itself. Its title would be unfortunate; its professional standards would compare unfavourably with those of the BBC, and its programme planning would not be co-ordinated with that of the BBC to give the viewer real alternatives. It would be an expensive redundancy.

This country has gained a good deal of prestige abroad by having the Third Programme in sound radio, which serves a valuable purpose for a limited number of people. It is often spoken of as educational, and it does of course transmit a great deal of material which can rightly be called educational, but it is so little received that its value as an educational medium is small. To my mind it is almost the antithesis of education as we broadcasters understand it. True broadcast education popularizes culture without debasing it and makes it a part of everyday life. This is no criticism of the Third Programme, which is a useful service to well-educated people, but I want to make the point that, as a model, it has nothing to offer to those of us who are genuinely interested in the greater use of television as an educational medium.

Those who are genuinely interested in more and better ETV for Britain, need to be very much on their guard against people, who for wholly different reasons, appear to be working for the same end. What we want is more *reception* of ETV by the people. This may involve more *production* and *transmission* of ETV, but that is not the object. The object is to educate, not to pump out educational material into the ether. Those who are not genuinely interested, but wish to give the appearance of being so, will tend to back projects which put fences around ETV, fences which they know the public will not climb. More ETV will be produced and transmitted; less will be received, but a channel, the existence of which is expected to be an embarrassment to commercial television, will be sterilized, and this is what they want. They don't want people in any quantity to be viewing on another BBC channel, because that would be bad for the advertising business. Another channel in the hands

EDUCATION AND INSTRUCTION

of the BBC would attract more viewers and expose them to education. These same viewers are wanted by commercial television for exposure to advertising. Education has one thing in common with advertising; it is not the quantity transmitted which matters; it is the amount of the exposure.

Now I must get on to the question of programmes for minorities. It is commonly held that it is a good thing to cater for minority interests in broadcasting. The BBC's sound services do a lot of it, but the sound networks are three in number with regional variants and longer hours throughout the day. There is much more room for them, and ample alternatives for people who do not share the particular minority tastes. Most people have minority interests, in addition to the interests they share with millions of others. It is quite possible for one man to be a keen follower of boxing, a lover of Tony Hancock, Jimmy Edwards, Harry Worth and Eric Sykes and a devoted viewer of news and current affairs programmes—all interests which he shares with millions of others—and at the same time to be a collector of Etruscan pottery and a breeder of rare moths—interests which he shares with only a very few. That part of a man's mind which carries 'minority interests' is the most unique part of him and may well be the most original and productive part. He wants information about these things, and he desires contact and exchange of views with others who share his special interests. A large number of specialized periodicals with small circulations are published to meet these needs, and societies exist to bring the enthusiasts together. I do not believe that this sort of thing has much to do with popular education, but it is often held to be a part of it. Whatever it is, it is an important facet of life, and one of the few movements of the human spirit away from the dreary uniformity of the commonplace.

BBC television with its single network has done practically nothing to meet small minority interests. There are too many of them, and too little space in which to display them, but in my day we gave a lot of thought to these things. What is a minority interest? How small or how technical has that interest to be before it comes outside the legitimate sphere of television? What sort of interests known to have only small followings would be permissible if the space could be found for them? My successor Kenneth Adam, when he was the Controller of Television Programmes, developed a policy with which I entirely agreed; he called it the concept of the 'Small Majority'. At first it seems like a contradiction of terms, but it is not so really. A small majority interest is one which is known to have only a small following at first but which is of such a nature that it could have a very large following. A case in point is show jumping. A few years ago only a rather select few knew anything about it or had any special taste for it, but as a result of exposure on BBC television it has become a large majority interest. The same is true of athletics, and it is on the way to being true of good music and the plastic arts. The fact that the BBC's relatively high proportion of educational material is not apparently keeping it in a permanent position of numerical inferiority to ITA is due, I think, to the fact that small majority interests are slowly but surely becoming large majority interests. In television terms this is how the educational process works. Interests, which are potential but not yet actual, are fed and thereby developed into actuality.

At the other extreme there remains the problem of the small minority interest which for one reason or another is destined always to remain small. It is unusually well served by other media of communication, and I doubt whether television can ever do very much about it. But there is a broad middle belt of minority interests, which at present are receiving less attention than they deserve, local affairs, commercial and financial matters, technical and scientific interests, guidance in 'Do It Yourself', gardening, agriculture and so on. There is a very wide range of material here which has not been altogether neglected but which could be expanded and enriched by the BBC when it has two channels. I suppose the most socially important sphere of minority interest is the local sphere, and a good deal more will be done here.

Whereas Educational Television (ETV) should be television's prime objective, Instructional Television (ITV as it is called in America) is a wholly different concept. Unfortunately they often get confused because of the loose way in which we use the word 'education' to cover a lot of different things. ITV is not quite broadcasting in the true sense; it is the use of electronic equipment as an aid to teachers in schools or universities, and it provides an extra facility for something which is there

EDUCATION AND INSTRUCTION

already. Instructional broadcasting began in sound radio in the nineteen twenties when Reith got the idea that it should be offered to the teaching profession in schools. They, the local educational authorities and the Ministry of Education itself, were at first very slow on the uptake, there being some fear that the radio might displace the teacher, and a good deal of doubt about how it could be usefully employed in the classroom. Reith very wisely insisted that this service must be run by the teaching profession for the teaching profession. The BBC would give up time on the air for it, pay for it and provide the technical know-how, but the BBC would not decide what subjects were to be taught or how they were to be presented. The BBC formed a body now known as the Central Council for School Broadcasting on which were represented the principal teaching interests. The Council was given its own staff and considerable funds for promoting the use of radio in schools. The BBC always felt that the costs of the council, a largely autonomous body, should be paid by the Ministry, but the Ministry has never been induced to pay them, so the BBC has to pay not only the costs of producing the programmes but also the costs of the council's work in the schools. After a somewhat uphill beginning the movement got under way and for many years radio has been an accepted adjunct to school teaching; there are not many British schools without it today.

The advent of television naturally raised the question of its possible use for the same purpose. The motion picture was becoming a valuable aid to teaching, so why not television? The BBC and the Council conducted some experiments, which were assessed and regarded as promising, and it was decided to start a regular service to schools in 1957. Associated Rediffusion TV made a similar decision at the same time. Granada came in later. So now both networks are doing ITV for schools; both seem to think it has a useful future and both have increased the output. So far progress is rather slow. There are known to be about 4,000 television receivers installed in schools, while 29,000 schools use radio. At the present rate it will be a long time before television catches up with radio.

The largest project in ITV for schools which I discovered in America is called 'The Midwest Program on Airborne Television Instruction'—MPATI for short. It is financed mainly by

TELEVISION: A CRITICAL REVIEW

the Ford Foundation and it is operated from a headquarters in one of the buildings of Purdue University, Lafayette, Indiana. It started operations on September 11, 1961, a few weeks before I got there, when I spent a whole morning with the President and members of his senior staff. They are a dedicated and enthusiastic group, who believe this is going to be one of the biggest things in school instruction, and they expect it to become financially self-supporting by contributions from the schools based on the number of their pupils. Like the BBC it is guided by a council of experts representing the educational authorities in the area it serves, which is a very large area comprising large parts of six states, Wisconsin, Michigan, Ohio, Indiana, Illinois and Kentucky, and its potential audience is said to be five million pupils in thirteen thousand schools and colleges.

The making of the programmes is put out to contract. Various firms in different parts of America make them under supervision, and record them on electronic tape. They are broadcast from a single transmitter mounted in an aeroplane, which also carries a machine for reproducing the taped programmes. It flies at 23,000 feet on a small circular course in all possible weather conditions. It is estimated that impossible weather conditions will not be more than about five per cent, and these are conditions in which many children find it difficult to get to school anyhow.

It is a remarkable project, designed to meet a very extraordinary set of circumstances. My first question was 'Why go to these lengths to provide televised instruction to people most of whom already have good reception from several ground stations?' The answer was that most of the ground stations, being commercial, would not give up time to a non-commercial object even in daytime. I was glad to be able to tell them that in my country both our networks, one of which is commercial, not only provide time for ITV, they make no charge for it and they even go so far as to pay for the programmes, which are made in their own studios. They do all this of their own volition, not because anybody pressed them into it. To an American educationalist the state of affairs in British television seems almost too good to be true.

I find in America generally a much greater enthusiasm for

instructional television than in Britain. This has a number of causes. It is partly a reaction against commercial television, and a wish to divert the medium into more socially useful channels, but it is also the result of a very difficult situation in most American universities. Unlike Britain where we put about four or five per cent of our young people through university, America is already putting through about twenty-five per cent, and their philosophy of education prompts them to raise the proportion without limit. This is creating a tremendous teacher problem; the numbers and therefore the quality of teachers is far below what is necessary for this tremendously ambitious programme. There is an atmosphere of bustle and urgency in most of the universities I visited.

The problem is most acute in California and Florida, where in addition to the natural growth of population, they are experiencing large-scale imigration from other parts of the United States. I met in Tallahassee the State Supervisor of Education for Florida, and asked him whether he really believed that television had an important and permanent role to play in classroom education in addition to its temporary role of compensating for the shortage of teachers. He was most emphatic in his view that it had.

The uses to which television is being put in American universities is interesting and varied. Some of them have transmitting stations of their own and broadcast cultural material to the surrounding population. Such stations are hopelessly underfinanced as a rule; they are generally operated by the teachers and students of the faculties of communications, which exist to qualify young people for jobs in broadcasting, journalism and advertising. Such faculties do not exist in British universities. The nearest equivalent here is the BBC's Staff Training School. Incidentally I have found American students in their spare time working as technicians for local commercial stations; on one occasion I was doing a studio interview for a commercial station and I found that my cameramen were university students to whom I had been lecturing a few hours earlier. I think a great deal of the impetus for television in American universities arises from the fact that the universities are already in the business as educators of young men and women who want to become professional broadcasters and who go to university to get an academic qualification in broadcasting. This interest naturally leads to experiments in the use of television as an aid to teaching subjects which have nothing to do with broadcasting, such as biology, history, mathematics and so on. The professors of communications and their students, who of course have electronic apparatus at their disposal, familiarize members of other faculties with the possibilities of the medium, and so it becomes accepted as a normal part of the machinery of instruction. Its acceptance is given further impetus by the excessive student-teacher ratio.

But this is not broadcasting as we understand it; it is the use of electronic apparatus for a limited instructional purpose within an academic institution. It may be done on 'open circuit', i.e. radiated from a wireless transmitter, or it may be done on 'closed circuit', i.e. carried by cable from the camera to the viewing screen. It is very often done on closed circuit. I gave a lecture to students and faculty of the Los Angeles State College last autumn, and I delivered my lecture before cameras in the college television studio, where I had a small audience with me, but I was assured that most of my audience were in lecture rooms, libraries and other places which were equipped with television receivers, connected by cable with my cameras. I hope they were. The uses of closed circuit television for instruction in surgery, dentistry, etc., are obvious, and are being developed.

The following facts were published in the Education Supplement of *The Saturday Review* in May, 1961. Though out of date now, they may give the reader some idea of current trends.

'1. At least 3,000,000 students in about 7,000 elementary and secondary schools throughout the nation are receiving part of their regular daily instruction by television.

2. Perhaps as many additional students are receiving televised "enrichment" programmes, which are not considered part of the regular curriculum but which nevertheless are regarded by teachers as valuable supplement to daily lessons.

3. About 250 colleges and universities are offering credit courses on television to about 250,000 students. In addition some 300 colleges and universities are offering credit for courses taught on "Continental Classroom", the nation-wide program broadcast from 6 to 7 a.m. five days a week over the NBC net-

EDUCATION AND INSTRUCTION

work.'

Things are moving so fast in American instructional television that I would expect the figures to be substantially larger by now. The third paragraph of the quotation refers to what I believe to be a successful contribution to instruction being made by one of the big three commercial networks—the National Broadcasting Company.

In our own country there is nothing to compare with this enthusiastic readiness to use television as an aid to instruction, and I think the reason, apart from our temperamental conservatism, is that we are not so short of teachers and we have no faculties of communications in our universities. I expect Instructional Television will make steady progress here but at a slower pace, and for some time to come will be used mainly in schools. If and when it becomes a major factor in British teaching, we shall have to face up to the question whether it should be provided by open circuit or closed circuit. Open circuit would mean setting aside a special network for it. This in turn would use up channels, which would lie idle in vacation time and at week-ends. There is another and even more serious disadvantage in the open circuit system. Unless we had a number of networks given up to instruction, which is unthinkable, we could have only one lesson at a time. The extensive use of television for instruction in universities and technical colleges would be impossible without a very large number of programmes being made available simultaneously, and this would be quite impossible on open circuit. I am sure that the future of instructional television lies in the closed circuit method, which in a limited area would carry a large number of lessons simultaneously. If I am right in this, instructional television in the more distant future will not be the business of the broadcasting authorities at all, but will become the business of the Educational Authorities.

Meanwhile the BBC and the ITA between them are offering a useful but limited instructional service for the schools, and I have no doubt they will go on doing it, but I do not believe that open circuit broadcasting, which is the sole business of these two authorities, is at all well adapted to the needs of higher teaching. The future lies with closed circuit transmission of instructional material initiated and financed by the educational authorities themselves. In this respect the Americans are so far ahead of us that their progress deserves the attention of anyone interested in teaching techniques.

The introduction of audio-visual aids into our universities and secondary schools is going to be one of the major revolutions of the twentieth century. The enormous increase in the number of students will soon make obsolete the lecturer in the class-room or the lecture theatre. University and school libraries will not be able to cope with the demand for reference books. At the same time knowledge is becoming more and more specialized, and the problem of how to get the information to the student will soon become insoluble unless we accept electronics as the solution. It is now possible to store vast quantities of information electronically and to make it available at a moment's notice on closed circuit to any student requiring it. The machinery for self-teaching already exists, and there need be no teacher shortage. The best teachers can be made to teach infinitely more students than they teach today; their lectures can be repeated *ad infinitum*. This is an immense subject; so revolutionary that at first it will meet with resistance, and possibly derision, from intrenched teaching interests.

This is not a book about teaching by electronics; it is about television broadcasting, but I want to make the point that teaching by electronic methods is something wholly different, and apart from, television broadcasting. In this country the educational authorities have, for too long, looked to the broadcasters to do the electronic job for them, but in fact the broadcasters can never do it except in the most rudimentary way. Now it is time for the educational authorities to explore the possibilities of modern techniques for themselves.

I cannot end this chapter without referring to a remarkable example of Instructional Television. For half an hour at a most popular time every night Italy's single network devotes itself to teaching the older people to read and write; I cannot imagine any way except television of giving literacy to millions of people who failed to acquire it in their youth.

CHAPTER 10

Global Television

SOUND radio has been a medium of instantaneous world-wide communication since its early days; it can be transmitted over very long distances on waves, which are reflected from the upper atmosphere, and it can be sent over telephone cables from the originating country to a local radio station in the receiving country and from there it can be rebroadcast to the people as part of the normal domestic service. There are no technical differences as between one country and any other which make this impossible or even difficult. The only problem experienced by some countries is how to keep unwelcome radio transmissions out. Sometimes they are unwelcome because they interfere with domestic programmes; sometimes, as in the case of Russia, because they convey messages which the government of the receiving country regards as damaging to its interests.

But in television the situation is entirely different; it is not, except in most unusual circumstances, a medium of direct communication between the broadcasting authority of one country and the people of another. Therefore as a weapon of foreign policy it is comparatively useless; it is essentially a domestic medium. Television authorities address themselves to their own people, and any foreign material which gets onto the domestic screen gets there because the domestic television authorities put it there.

A domestic television service without any foreign material in it is narrow and parochial, and failing in one of its most important functions, which is to be for the people a window on the world. During my time in BBC television about fifteen per cent of our programme material was of foreign make. Some of it was 'live'; that is to say it was transmitted instantaneously, and some of it was imported as records on film or tape. Of the fifteen per cent ten was American. (I always hoped for a higher proportion of non-American foreign material.) These figures apply only to foreign *made* material, but in addition the BBC itself makes large numbers of filmed programmes in other countries especially for showing on the British domestic screen.

But the BBC had always wanted to be able to include in its programmes living instantaneous pictures of events as they were taking place in other countries, just as it had been doing for years in respect of events taking place in Britain, but until about ten years ago there were serious technical difficulties which had proved insuperable. All the receiving sets in Britain are made to receive pictures transmitted on 405 picture lines and no other; European and Soviet programmes are transmitted on 625 lines, French on 819, American on 525. Indeed no other country in the world uses the British standard of 405, and so we were faced with the prospect of being isolated for ever from the outside world in terms of live television; we could neither receive from nor send to other countries. Photographic film was our only link with the world, which was intolerable.

The problem was how to convert instantaneously a picture transmitted say in France on 819 lines to a picture receivable in Britain on 405 lines, and, what was more, how to do it without serious degradation of the picture quality.

We made a start in 1950 with the goodwill and active help of the French television authorities by landing BBC mobile cameras at Calais, and from there on August the 27th we broadcast a two-hour programme about Calais to the British people. This was the world's first live television broadcast from a foreign country. It inspired imaginations. It opened up in men's minds the prospect of unlimited development, but it solved no problems, because the programme was not transmitted by French cameras on the French line standard, but by British cameras on the British line standard, and the French could not receive it themselves because it was not transmitted on their standard. In short it was not true international television, but it was a start.

It led directly to a fruitful partnership between British and French television engineers, who were determined to solve the difficult technical problem of conversion. Within two years they had so far succeeded that the French were able, in July, 1952, to mount fourteen programmes in a period of two weeks from Paris, all of which were converted to the British line standard at the coast and transmitted instantaneously to British viewers through the BBC's own stations. The nut was cracked at last. Of course the picture quality was far from perfect at first, but since then great improvements have been made. In 1953 the coronation of Queen Elizabeth II was broadcast throughout France, Holland and eastwards as far as Berlin. The next year Italian television brought the Seven Hills of Rome into the homes of eight European countries. In 1960 the Olympic Games in Rome were seen instantaneously by vast audiences from Warsaw to the Pyrenees. In 1961 we saw Moscow's reception of Major Gagarin and the Moscow May Day Parade. But these are just a few of the highlights of international television. Today hundreds of live programmes are interchanged between European countries every year; it has become a matter of routine.

International television began in 1952 as a purely Anglo-French affair, but there was every intention to extend its scope as quickly as possible. Other European countries were invited to participate as soon as their internal television links were ready. The early programmes from Calais and Paris and a larger scale experimental interchange between eight countries in 1954 were the result of arrangements improvised to serve a special need. After the 1954 experiment it was clear to those taking part that some more formal framework was needed, within which programme projects could be discussed and technical arrangements co-ordinated. The countries which had joined in the experiment were all members of the European Broadcasting Union, and the Union was approached to take over the organization of programme exchanges; the acceptance of this task by the Union marked the official beginning of 'Eurovision' as we know it today. An international programme committee and two technical working parties were formed; a new office was opened in Geneva to act as a clearing house for programme offers made by member countries, and to pass on information to the Eurovision Technical Centre in Brussels.

Now there are eighteen member countries—Britain, France, Germany, the Netherlands, Italy, Belgium, Denmark, Norway, Switzerland, Sweden, Finland, Austria, Luxembourg, Monaco, Spain, Yugoslavia, Portugal and Algeria. (The inclusion of

Algeria shows that the movement has already begun to reach over to the African continent.) Eurovision, in addition to being a practical working organization, has become a sort of club of like-minded men and women, who share a general sense of what television can contribute to European life. They are overwhelmingly non-commercial in their approach to the medium, the whole tradition of European broadcasting being based on the public service concept. However, it would be unrealistic for them to ignore the existence of commercialized television, and so ITA has become a full member, though its participation in Eurovision programmes is much less than the BBC's. Broadcasting organizations outside the range of Eurovision can be associate members and many have joined on this basis—the major American networks, the American educational stations and television organizations as far away as Australia and Japan.

The programme committee meets at regular intervals in different countries, which means that delegates from each broadcasting organization have the chance to see how television is developing in other countries. Inevitably there are differences in the scale of these organizations, while some are young and not yet well equipped, others are mature services with backgrounds of considerable achievement. But all contribute to the work of the committee, and all are anxious to increase the number of serious programmes which are offered for exchange. The language difficulty is an obvious one, but communication by television does not usually depend so heavily on the spoken word as radio does, and a commentary in one's own language is often all that is needed. Another difficulty is presented by the complications of international copyright and performers' rights, but many of these have been resolved by the Union's Legal Committee.

More subtle, however, are the difficulties of devising programmes which can simultaneously appeal to audiences with different social, cultural and educational backgrounds. The successful television programme is usually devised with a particular domestic audience and a particular object in mind. The fact that all viewers are Europeans is not in itself sufficient, except in limited ways, to provide a homogeneous audience, and the Committee is always striving for programme forms which will transcend the divisions amongst the audience. My own opinion is that the most successful material for international dissemination is the public event, of which a great number have already found their way on to the screens of all European countries. We have had the Coronation of Pope John XXIII, state visits by heads of state including of course our own Queen to other countries, the funeral of Toscanini in Milan, the weddings of Prince Albert of the Belgians and of Princess Grace of Monaco, the State Opening of Parliament, the Calvin Anniversary Celebrations in Geneva, a conversation between President Eisenhower and Mr Macmillan in London, and Mr Krushchev's press conference in Paris. And then there have been a vast number of sporting contests of all kinds, skiing, football, athletics, tennis, show jumping, skating, dancing and motor racing. There have been international song contests and international entertainment contests. An unusual use for Eurovision was found in early 1961 when three countries, France, Italy and Yugoslavia, broadcast scenes of a total eclipse of the sun as it passed in rapid succession over their three countries. I believe that the most important use of this powerful international medium is the live reporting of important or interesting events while they are actually taking place. This is the real stuff of television; it is unique to the medium; it gives the viewer a sense of participation which nothing else, short of actually being present, can give.

But an international television network has other important uses. It makes possible the rapid transference of news film over long distances. The visual part of television news is nearly always shot with photographic cameras (electronic cameras, and their accompanying gear, are much larger, clumsier and less mobile), the resulting films having to be processed and transported to the television station for inclusion in the news. Film shot in distant lands for BBC news is normally taken to the nearest airport, flown on the next regular plane to London Airport. There may be fogs, ice, snow, strikes, delays due to mechanical faults and traffic blocks between London Airport and the Television Centre. Sometimes there may even be delays with the customs. Thus visual material from other countries can take too long to get on to the screens for which it is intended, but the Eurovision network comes to the rescue and cuts out nearly all delays. One of the earliest examples was on the occasion of the death of the late Pope at Castel Gandolfo outside Rome. Film of the scenes outside the Castel was taken physically to Rome, processed there and, instead of being put on to the next plane for London, it was handed over to the Italian television authorities, who transmitted it as an instantaneous electronic process over the Eurovision network to London, where it was recorded by the BBC and broadcast to the British people at the next opportunity. British viewers saw the event within three hours of it taking place. By now the method has become commonplace, and instantaneous transmissions of news film between members of Eurovision is becoming an ordinary part of the day's business.

But much of the news film, which finds its way on to the screens of all countries, is shot far outside the range of the Eurovision network; Africa, India, the Far and the Near East, are frequently in the news. Even here Eurovision can help. For instance Rome is a main junction for planes arriving from these distant parts. In 1959 planes were arriving in Rome carrying newsfilm of President Eisenhower's world tour—film shot in India, Greece and other points on the tour. The film was offloaded at Rome and transmitted instantaneously through the Eurovision network for showing in the domestic services of the member countries.

The significance of Eurovision is that it was the first, and is still the most highly developed of international television networks. But it is not the only one now. The Soviet Union, which was relatively slow in developing television, is now going ahead with some speed, and either has, or soon will have, a hundred television stations. Czechoslovakia, Poland and Hungary have theirs. Internal television circuits, let alone international ones, take time to establish, especially where great distances are involved, but all this is being done, and an East European international network is growing up with the title of 'Intervision'. The first link between Eurovision and Intervision was forged in April, 1961, by BBC, Finnish and Russian engineers, who succeeded in linking Moscow through Tallin with Helsinki in Finland; Helsinki was linked with Stockholm and the Eurovision network. Thus Moscow's reception of the world's first astronaut, Major Gagarin, was seen in Britain on the first live television link ever to be forged between Western and Eastern Europe.

GLOBAL TELEVISION

The Soviet Union has taken a few live programmes from Britain in the reverse direction, notably the Trooping of the Colour later the same year. Co-operation between Eurovision and Intervision will soon cease to present major technical problems. If there are problems (and I guess there will be) they will be political.

Our biggest problem has been, and still is, the westward expansion of the international network; the Atlantic Ocean has so far been an insuperable barrier. Normally radiated television transmissions will not carry further than a hundred miles or so, and the capacity of the transatlantic cables is nothing like sufficient to carry moving pictures. Therefore no live television has ever spanned the Atlantic.* With one exception which I shall describe later, all television material from the other side is recorded on film or tape and flown or shipped across the ocean. In a sense it is all old stuff by the time it is shown on the screen. Neither we nor the Americans nor the Canadians have ever seen a programme or an event from the other side while it was actually taking place. This has been a serious defect in our system of communications, and our peculiarly close relations with these two great Transatlantic peoples makes the situation doubly regrettable.

The first successful attempt to mitigate the defect was made by the BBC's engineers in 1959. They invented a device known as 'Cable Film', which takes advantage of the fact that the transatlantic cables, lacking the capacity to carry moving pictures at normal speed, can carry them if they are very much slowed down. Cable Film transmits a picture through the cable at one-hundredth of its normal speed. It is recorded as it comes out at the other end and the record is then used at normal speed in the domestic service of the receiving country. An event in America lasting one minute can be broadcast to the British people one hour and forty minutes later, which is much better than the ten or twelve hours it would take to send the news-film by air. It is useful only for short items such as normally occur in news bulletins; longer items take so long to put through Cable Film that it is better to use air transport anyway. A Cable Film machine has been provided for the National Broadcasting Company of America, with whom the BBC has a news

* Written before Telstar went into orbit.

agreement, and there are regular exchanges of news items between these two organizations. The first use of Cable Film was in 1959 when the Queen and the President opened the St Lawrence Seaway.

But this is not live television comparable with what has been going on in Europe for years. For this we need some quite new method of transmission, and we know what it is going to be—active communication earth satellites.

At the time of writing this chapter no such satellites are yet in orbit, but there is every chance of their being so before the book gets into print. It is believed that it will be possible to transmit live television pictures from a ground station in Europe to a satellite orbiting over the middle of the Atlantic at say three thousand miles above the earth. A receiver in the satellite will pick up the picture, and a transmitter in the same satellite will retransmit it to a ground receiving station on the American continent. It will work equally well in either direction. This is what we all believe, but it has not yet been tried. Ground stations have already been built in Cornwall, France and America. But the first satellite has not yet been put into orbit. A stationary satellite—that is to say one which remained permanently over the same point on the Earth's surface—would have to be very high, probably too high for television transmission. So I expect we shall need a procession of satellites moving round the Earth at a lower level, travelling at carefully calculated intervals so that at least one is above the horizon at any given moment. As soon as one begins to set, the transmission would be shifted to the next satellite, which would then be coming up from the other horizon.

This sort of thing is immensely expensive, and to the best of my belief America will provide most of the investment. As a comprehensive means of communication carrying telephone, telegraph, radio and television traffic it may pay its way, but television alone could not possibly support an enterprise of this magnitude. If the Atlantic is successfully spanned this year, we shall in due course expect the Pacific and Indian oceans to be similarly spanned, and then global television will begin to become a reality.

It is one thing to achieve a world-wide system of pictorial communication; quite another to decide for what purposes that system shall be used. The rates per minute for transatlantic television circuits will be very high, and none but wealthy television authorities will be able to afford them very often. Long distance transmission eastwards or westwards comes up against big time differences, which could be cushioned by recording for later use by the receiving countries, but that would destroy the element of immediacy. If we are going to sacrifice immediacy because of the time difference, we might consider another and less costly way than satellites of getting the material across. A regular service of jet aircraft travelling at one or two thousand miles an hour would more than make up for the time difference. Films or tapes do not weigh much and the freight charges would be nothing compared with the cost of satellite vision circuits. But I hope there will be an increasing number of televised events on both sides of the Atlantic, which will be so important as to outweigh the inconvenience of the time difference.

I spoke a lot about these prospects on my recent American tour. Up to the present American television has been rather parochial; with a few notable exceptions, the people in the business have little desire to extend the scope of television, or treat it as a medium of international communication. The idea is a new one in America and very little is known there about the developments in Europe over the last ten years. I was often asked whether I thought global live television would be used mainly for entertainment, and I frequently met the belief that it would be a wonderful world-wide medium for advertising American goods. I was a little depressed by the prevalence of these ideas, and I always replied by saying that immediacy was so unimportant both in entertainment and in advertising that, if I were an American advertiser, I should save my money and use cheaper and more old-fashioned methods of getting my material across the Ocean.

I must confess to certain misgivings about the use of the global television network when we get it. So far we have had a lot of experience within the European group and a little experience of co-operation with Soviet Russia. Within Western Europe we have enjoyed uniquely favourable conditions for many years. The countries in this group share a more or less common culture, and even though their languages are different their thoughts and their basic assumptions have much in common. This community of interests applies with even greater force between Britain and the United States, except in television. Europe has one conception of television. The United States has another. The fact that nearly all European television authorities are free from contracts with advertisers gives them a degree of flexibility, which is extremely important to successful co-operation. It is not at all easy for a television service wholly dependent on advertising revenue and with long-term advertising contracts to honour, to change its schedules, at very short notice, to accommodate programmes which reflect current events either at home or abroad.

But there are occasional exceptions. In November, 1961, I was staying in an hotel in Beverly Hills, California, when a series of devastating bush fires broke out all round me. My hotel fortunately was in no danger, but the smoke and dust from the fires was coming in at my bedroom windows, and I was near enough to know that something very serious was going on around me. There was a sense of anxiety; refugees, whose homes were being reduced to ashes, were coming into the hotel for asylum, and nobody knew whether the fires would be checked that night or whether vast built-up areas would be destroyed and perhaps tens or hundreds of thousands rendered homeless. I turned to television and found that two of the Los Angeles stations, both independent, had in fact scrapped their evening schedules, and had sent out their mobile cameras and reporting teams to report the battle between the fires and the fire fighters. Next day the *Los Angeles Times* in a very prominent article praised the two independent stations for their public spirit and enterprise, ending by saying that it was a pity it took a major public disaster to bring television to life, the implication being that it was very unusual for commercial television to behave in that way. And the reason is perfectly clear—lack of flexibility due to advertising contracts. If television is employed as a mere advertising medium it is very difficult and very expensive to bring it to life at short notice, and a commercial station, which does so, risks losing a lot of money. Thus the system discourages the live reporting of sudden, unexpected or irregular events, and yet these, above all else, are the unique stuff of television. They are likely to be the principal stuff of global television. I believe the live reporting of the Californian fires was a purely local enterprise, not seen by people outside California, but it would have made good material even for the British screen, although it would have been breakfast time here. Some very well-known film stars were being burnt out, and anything that happens to them is news.

I believe the full possibilities of Global television can only be grasped if we think of it as primarily a news medium. One of the weaknesses of all television organizations is their tendency to isolate news from the rest of their operations, and thus to confine news to short regular bulletins of verbal information generally supported by filmed pictures. This is particularly characteristic of commercial television, whose main business is the fulfilment of contracts with advertisers on fixed time-tables. The unexpected, unique or irregular is the enemy of good business in commercial television.

At this point I must pay a tribute to the news and public affairs divisions of the American networks, especially the Columbia Broadcasting System and the National Broadcasting Company, who for many years have done first-class work in this field. The former produced Edward R. Murrow, now unhappily cut off from broadcasting because of his duties as head of the Federal Government's information office. Murrow was the doyen of the world's broadcasting commentators, as well known and respected abroad as he was at home. Both these networks have devoted some of their resources and some of their less profitable time slots to showing the world to the American people, and the result has been the very cream of American broadcasting. The BBC has been proud to reproduce on its own screen many of the public affairs programmes of these two American networks. But in commercial television this sort of thing has to be the Cinderella; it must accommodate itself to the main business of the network, which is to broadcast the advertisements, and the canned programmes which are inseparable from the advertisements, at fixed times according to contract. The vast bulk of American television, especially at the best viewing hours, is this and almost nothing else. One of its worst features is its appalling rigidity; its shackles are welded on so tight that it can hardly move. If by some divine dispensation it could happen that the world's most important and significant events could always occur every Tuesday at 8.0 p.m. Eastern

Standard Time and last for 24½ minutes precisely with 'natural breaks' they could become an important ingredient in American television. But unhappily they are seldom regular, not always predictable and never 24½ minutes long with 'natural breaks'. So we come to the question—how can an efficient machine for selling goods be, at the same time, an efficient window on the world?

This question becomes one of major importance to Europeans as soon as transatlantic live television arrives. The principal television authorities on both sides of the ocean will become increasingly dependent on each other for the supply of live broadcasts of important and significant events. Europe has already gone far in this direction; its major television authorities, free from the shackles of advertising contracts, are organized through Eurovision and Intervision to supply each other, and there would be no difficulty in their supplying transatlantic countries as soon as the satellites are working. But will the contracts with their sponsors permit the American networks to use our material or to supply us in sufficient quantity with the kind of live material we shall want from them? I don't know the answer to this question; but I do know that flexibility and enterprise are vitally important to the success of Global Television and these are qualities that are not easy to exercise in the straight-jacket of an advertising machine. I should like to see more scope, more resources, more of everything put into the News and Public Affairs divisions of the American networks, because these are the people who most nearly speak the language and think the thoughts of public service broadcasting.

It is one thing for the human race, with its prolific ingenuity, to devise a global system of visual communications; it is quite another to use it fully and wisely for the enlightenment of the peoples of the world. The latter job will fall squarely on the shoulders of the world's television authorities. I expect there will have to be an official international body of television broadcasters to provide the machinery for exchange, and we can only hope they will have more in mind than the policies of their respective governments or the sale of their country's goods. Global television will be largely wasted unless it is used to bring truth into the people's homes.

CHAPTER 11

Canned Television

THE expression 'Canned Programmes' is often used in a derogatory sense to describe material of foreign origin, the showing of which robs native artists of employment. It is called canned because it can only be imported in recorded form and packed in cans for protection against physical damage, but in fact a very high proportion of programmes shown in all countries are prerecorded and canned whether they be foreign or home produced. It is done for a variety of reasons. The economic use of studios often demands a production schedule different from the showing schedule and this means producing in advance and canning for subsequent showing; the interval may be no more than a few hours, or it may be very much longer. Prerecording is sometimes used to achieve a more polished production, because it enables a producer to repeat passages if he is not quite satisfied with them; this may be good art but it is bad economy. Canning of programmes whether prerecorded or not is done for purposes of repetition or reference or both. But above all recording and canning are done with the object of selling the programmes to other people.

Here I must attempt to explain a few of the complexities of the television industry. The film industry is a useful analogy with its producers, distributors and exhibitors. Basically a television service is an exhibitor, analogous to a cinema. It is perfectly possible to run a television service from a single transmitting station with no studio, no cameras and none of the apparatus of production; all that is needed is a piece of apparatus analogous to the projector to reproduce recorded programmes bought in cans from other sources. This is what a cinema does. I do not know of any television service in the world, which is quite as simple as this, but it is possible and it may exist. It would be television confining itself exclusively to its basic role of exhibitor.

But, unlike a cinema, a television service nearly always produces some part of the material it exhibits. It may be only a very small part. In practice a television service is always an exhibitor and generally a producer, large, small or very small according to circumstances. Just as I know of no service which produces nothing for itself, so I know of no service which produces everything for itself. Thus there is some buying and selling of programme material between television services throughout the world. But material produced electronically by television is subject to the same limitations of differential line and electrical standards, which I described in connection with international live television. The material, in this case canned material, must be converted to the standards of the buying country before it can be used, just as live material must be so converted. This limitation, which is not quite hundred per cent solved even now, has kept international trade in canned programmes produced by television within relatively small dimensions. It is an odd fact that, for purely technical reasons, it has been difficult for television services to trade their own canned products with each other, whereas there has never been the smallest technical difficulty in the film industry, with its more cumbersome and old-fashioned photographic process, trading its products with every television service in the world. Photography, not being an electronic process, is unaffected by differences in line and electrical standards. So it is not surprising that the world's demand for canned television programmes has been satisfied mainly by the film producers of Hollywood.

At this point I ought to give the reader some notion of the magnitude of the demand. The British viewer is accustomed to his own two networks, one of which, the BBC, exhibits about ten per cent of Hollywood material, the other, the ITA, exhibits about fourteen per cent. It is not widely understood in this country that these percentages are very small by comparison with most other countries. The latest comparable American figure to reach me was an average for the three national networks; they show eighty-five per cent of Hollywood material. In so far as a television service shows Hollywood material it is acting only as an exhibitor. (We all have sources of canned ready-made material other than Hollywood, but they are relatively small.) A high percentage of Hollywood material shown by a television service is a fair guide to the smallness of its own producing operation, and vice versa. Thus it can be inferred that the BBC's producing operation is a very large one. (It is incidentally the largest in the world.) It can be inferred that the producing operations of the American networks are very small. It is not so easy to get figures for other countries, but a valuable source of information is the BBC producer Richard Cawston who in 1961 made two world tours in connection with a documentary programme he made on television throughout the world. He probably has a more comprehensive knowledge of the state of the industry today than any other man, and he paints an extremely gloomy picture of conditions in most countries outside Europe. Of course he did not visit every one of the eighty countries which now have television, but he took a pretty fair sample. He found little of value on the American continent North or South, except in Canada, especially in French Canada, and in Cuba. Japan is perhaps the most progressive of all. Tokio has three channels in colour and three in black and white. Colour is used even in televised lessons for children in school. In Japan some real effort is made to use television creatively, and in a Japanese way. Apart from the United Arab Republic, which is very progressive, the Near East, the Far East and Africa are mainly extensions of Hollywood. When Cawston was in Thailand they were showing 'Victory at Sea', 'Victory Through Air Power', and all the gangster films. As he went up the klongs and rivers with the houses on stilts, he heard broadsides and pistol shots coming across the otherwise peaceful waters, mixed in with American voices, and nothing else. Cawston went upstairs in some of these buildings, took his shoes off and squatted on the floors. The people were just watching. They prefer Westerns and cowboy programmes; detective and private eye stories are not so easy to follow in a language you don't understand.

This astonishing state of affairs arises from the ease with which anybody can buy, on favourable financial terms, a television transmitter and a telecine (the machine which reproduces canned programmes). The possession of a television station has become an important status symbol, signifying a modern independent state, and as such it is attractive to governments. A television station, like a cow, can be bought on reasonable terms, but the big expense comes in feeding the animal; it is the making of indigenous programmes which demands big resources of money, skill and talent, whereas the mere exhibiting of ready-made canned material from abroad makes no demands at all. It is a constant source of wonder to me that states can be satisfied with so empty a symbol, which suggests dependence rather than independence, but so it is in many cases. I find it difficult to understand the desire to possess a medium of communication unless you have something to communicate and the means to do it. But where these are lacking, the programmes are virtually put out to contract, and foreign contract at that. However deplorable all this may be from the point of view of the television industry in general and the affected countries in particular, it provides a magnificent business opportunity for anyone able to take over, in whole or in part, the programming of other countries' television stations. Hollywood was not slow to appreciate this fact, and today a very high proportion (I have heard fifty per cent and even seventy per cent mentioned) of television programmes shown throughout the non-communist world, excluding Europe, are these standardized Hollywood products, made to the specification of the American domestic advertising sponsor.

There are many reasons why Hollywood has so predominant a position in the world market; experience, competence, climate all play their part; but the chief reason is that the cost of making entertainment programmes by the old photographic process is so high that the entire world market without the United States is insufficient to cover the costs of production. The American television market is the first essential, and Hollywood has it. Having sold a product on the American market, or made it to measure for that market, it can be sold to other countries for what it will fetch. I hear of one country which can buy Hollywood programmes at £12 each, if it takes fifty at a time, or £7 each if it buys in packages of two hundred. Those programmes cost anything between £15,000 and £25,000 each to produce.

A visit to Hollywood's programme factories is a memorable and illuminating experience. I have done it twice; the more recent visit being made in October, 1961. The biggest factory is that of the Music Corporation of America (MCA), which covers a total area of 400 acres. 150 acres are built up and the rest is mountainous desert suitable for shooting Westerns and the like. The built-up area is fantastic; it is a conglomeration of every conceivable type of street scene built in plaster. As there is no rain the plaster façades are more or less permanent. The visitor wandering round may find himself in Piccadilly and turning a corner he is on the waterfront of a French fishing village; a few yards further and he is in the Chinese quarter of San Francisco to be followed by an impenetrable tropical jungle; and so it goes on—a dazzling panorama of make-believe—providing the visual background to almost any story the American advertiser may decide to launch on the world. Real trees are brought in and sprayed with green paint, because they photograph better that way and last longer. In the mountainous part of the estate I was shown a rocky gorge, used for battles between Indians and white men. One side of the gorge was natural rock, the other plaster.

A large number of studios, or 'Stages' as they are called, are there for shooting indoor scenes. A factory such as this makes several dozen series simultaneously, mostly thirtyniners. A half-hour episode takes three days to shoot; a one-hour episode takes five days. The organization is superb. Nearly every series is registered as a separate company and financed by anybody willing to put up the money. The timing of the production process is exact, and the efficiency of the whole business is most impressive. It is the nearest thing to standardized mass-production that one is likely to find in the entertainment business. It is sobering to stand in the middle of all this and to remind oneself that these mass-produced telefilms are destined to become the principal diet of most of the world's television viewers.

I have always been very much concerned about this worldwide traffic in television entertainment. Its products are of only limited importance to the BBC as an exhibitor, but the making and supplying of such material to other countries seemed to me to be something which the British film industry ought to be doing. While Hollywood will always have the lion's share of the trade, there seems every reason for Britain to make a bid for its own share, but this means investing not less than half a million pounds in each series of thirty-nine programmes. Most of that money would be lost unless a national sale to an American sponsor were secured. British film makers are, rightly, unwilling to take the risk unless they can get, in advance of production, a guaranteed acceptance from an American commercial sponsor, but that has proved so difficult that the British film industry for many years played no part in the making of entertainment programmes for television. It always seemed to me that a start might be made if the film industry could be given the financial and professional backing of British television, and furthermore, if every project were undertaken in partnership with an American interest. A start was made on these lines both by the BBC and by Associated Television (one of the big four contractors to the ITA). Probably the most successful British series in the early days was ATV's 'Robin Hood'; the BBC followed with 'The Third Man', which was sponsored by a big firm of American brewers, and is still doing well in America and other countries. Recently more filmed series have been undertaken with the financial backing of British television; for instance 'Zero One' is being made by MGM London with the BBC's financial backing.

They are made in series of thirty-nine episodes to fit the requirements of the commercial sponsor, who needs a programme a week at a fixed time for nine months with repeats during the three summer holiday months. Series of this kind must be designed to support a year's advertising campaign, and each episode must be tailored to a precise length with natural breaks for the commercials. Such programmes are shown for entertainment in Britain, but in America they are primarily vehicles for advertising. They must always be shown in America to recover their costs, after which they are offered all over the world at prices the purchasers can afford to pay.

Now the British film industry is in the international television programme business, and some of their products are being seen shown in many of the eighty countries with television stations, which is satisfactory as far as it goes, but I hope it will go much further.

It may come as a surprise to the reader to learn that the most prolific producer of television programmes in the world is not the film industry, not even Hollywood, it is the BBC. This authority owns and operates programme producing plants in

CANNED TELEVISION

many of the principal cities of Britain. Its Television Centre at Shepherd's Bush, London, with seven major studios and some smaller ones, will, when finished, have cost about £15,000,000, while its total investment in production plant is much higher. The BBC makes for its own use about 3,000 hours of television programme material every year; a very high figure indeed. If we add to this the considerable productive resources of the ITA's contracting companies, we reach the conclusion that the British television industry is no mere exhibitor; it is also the world's largest producer of television programmes.

This raises the question why British television with its big lead in production should lag so far behind Hollywood as a supplier to the world market. The short answer is that Hollywood uses the photographic process, while the television industry uses the electronic process; but for the benefit of the uninitiated reader I must explain why this makes such an important difference. The electronic camera translates a scene into electrical impulses, which are transmitted to the viewer's home receiver as electrical impulses. The set receives the impulses and retranslates them back into the original scene, which appears as a picture on the screen. The whole picture is never on the screen at any one moment of time; it is continuously being built up, but the process is so much more rapid than the reactions of human eye that the eye is deceived into thinking the whole picture is always there. The building up process is not detected, and the eye is fooled. A photograph is quite different because the whole picture is there, and if you want a moving photographic picture you show one whole photograph after another in rapid succession. The Hollywood product is a series of whole photographs printed onto a reel of film, and technically it is a much simpler product. From the point of view of international trade it has one enormous advantage; it can be exhibited by any television service in the world easily and without loss of picture quality.

The problem with the electronic process has been how to capture that insubstantial picture; how to freeze it onto some kind of a record which can be taken out of its can at a later date and exhibited by somebody's television service without loss of picture quality. If the electronic producer can achieve this, he has something valuable to sell; if he can't achieve it, he has not.

The television industry has made two approaches to the problem of recording electronic pictures. The first, known here as Telerecording (Kinescope in America), transfers the electronic picture on to photographic film; the second, known everywhere as Videotape recording, transfers the electronic impulses onto magnetic tape. In one case you have a canned reel of film, in the other a canned reel of magnetic tape, which could be an article of international trade, if the purchaser could exhibit it with as little difficulty and loss of quality as he experiences with photographic film. In these matters the would-be vendors of electronic programmes were for a long time at a disadvantage in competition with the vendors of photographic programmes; their canned products were not so easy to exhibit.

Videotape recording has been perfected by the Ampex Corporation of California, and British television is almost entirely equipped with Ampex machines. For domestic use they are superb; the reproduction is practically indistinguishable from the original, but the tapes are not exportable without being put through the conversion process. This arises from the fact that Videotape recording reproduces the line standards and the electrical frequency standards of the original picture. As every country in the world has a line standard different from ours, every export on Videotape from Britain must first be converted. There is another obstacle to the export of programmes on Videotape; the Ampex machines needed for exhibiting the taped programmes are expensive, and it will be a long time before the more impecunious stations of the world can afford them.

So telerecording is still the most commonly used method of capturing and recording electronic programmes for export. For several years after its introduction its quality of reproduction was imperfect. The Americans used it to a limited extent, but they did not trouble to perfect it; they gave it a bad name and dropped it, when Videotape recording came in. Their requirements are totally different from ours; recording for them is mainly a device for overcoming the time differences within their own country. They do not export many electronic programmes. It is not surprising that their television industry switched over to Videotape, which for purely domestic purposes is unrivalled, but any country wishing to export electronic programmes on a large scale cannot afford to ignore Telerecording; for several

CANNED TELEVISION

more years it is likely to be the principal medium. It has always been so important to the BBC, as an exporter, that BBC engineers have devoted much time and money to the development and perfection of telerecording. They have succeeded to such a degree that the BBC's 'An Age of Kings', shown on television in most of the principal cities of America, is widely acclaimed there as one of the more important landmarks in American television. The BBC's improved telerecording made it possible. In 1960 the BBC exported 1,250 canned programmes; in 1961 the figure was 2,500. These figures are small by comparison with Hollywood, but they will grow. The 'Inspector Maigret' series was another electronic production made by the BBC with an eye to export.

Unfortunately a large proportion of Britain's overseas television customers are in the advertising straight-jacket, their requirements are stereotyped to series of thirty-nine episodes of precise length with natural breaks. These are what the sponsor wants, and he controls most of the market, especially the all-important American market. British television itself exhibits a few 'thirtyniners', some of American origin, but British programming on the whole is far more varied and flexible. Many of the BBC's best products are not saleable to sponsors precisely because they do not conform to the stereotyped pattern of sponsored television; for instance the dramatization of a Dickens' novel cannot be stretched out to thirty-nine episodes; the number of episodes and the length of each arises from the nature of the material, not from the business needs of Madison Avenue.

I have tried, with the generous help of Sir Norman Kipping, the Director General of the Federation of British Industries, to propagate the notion that British manufacturing firms might sponsor British television programmes, on commercial stations in other countries; thus we might kill two birds with one stone. Full sponsorship on an American network would probably be beyond the means of most British firms, but on the television of other countries it should be possible. I hope the idea will develop.

There is hardly a country in the world so dependent on the export of its manufactures as Britain. Exported canned television programmes may not have much direct affect on the balance of payments, but indirectly they have; whether they are sponsored by British firms or not, they are constant reminders of our existence, our standards of living and thinking and the wide range of our goods. The world demand for imported canned television programmes will persist for many years, and it is especially important for Britain to get as large a share of the trade as possible.

There is one other kind of canned programme, which has played a small part in British television and a much bigger part in many other countries; I refer to the big feature film made for theatrical showing in cinema houses. The British film producers and exhibitors have always been resolutely opposed to these films being shown on television at all; they have argued that showing them on the television screen keeps people away from the cinema. It is the same old argument which in the course of forty years the BBC has met from all sorts of interests. Churches, newspapers, theatres, sporting promoters—all in their time have claimed to be damaged by broadcasting and sought to withhold their products from it. In almost every case their fears have proved groundless, and in some cases hostility has dissolved into enthusiastic support. However, broadcasting in this country has never tried to ride roughshod over other interests; it has always sought to reassure the fearful and make agreements embodying compromises.

In the case of the film industry the road was long and painful; both before and after the war no cinema films were available to BBC television. When I became Director of BBC Television in 1956 negotiations with the film industry had been going on for a long time, and one of my first duties was to attend a lunch at the Dorchester with Sir Ian Jacob, my Director General. Our hosts were the leaders of the film industry, and Mr John Davis of the Rank Organization was in the chair. Over the lunch table we reached an agreement that the BBC would be allowed to show each year a very small number of cinema films, British or foreign, and these would be made available to us by the industry. In fact no films were made available at a realistic price, and at a return lunch about a year later we cancelled the agreement by mutual consent, which left the situation wide open again. The BBC still had no films, though we had shown our willingness to submit to a very close restriction in deference to the fears of the British film industry. The agreement had proved abortive and the BBC was on its own again, so we were free to act independently, and shortly afterwards I bought from my friend Nicolas Reissini of Robin International the British rights for seven years in the hundred best films picked from the famous RKO collection. These were all American films. At a later date Paul Adorian, Managing Director of Associated Rediffusion TV bought the television rights in fifty British films and invited the BBC to take a half share in them, which we did. So now both British networks are in a position to show cinema films, British and foreign.

Regrettably the film industry is still not reconciled to it. They had their chance to place very severe restrictions on television, and they let it go. Perhaps they did not know, or thought we did not know, that many hundreds of old cinema films had passed out of the hands of the industry altogether and were available for purchase in America. The film and television industries are natural allies. They could do so much to help each other, and it is a pity that there does not exist between them a sensible understanding on this question of cinema films for television.

Most cinema films are immensely costly to make and no reputable television authority wants to show them before they have earned all the money they are capable of earning in the cinema. But even after they have ceased to have any earning capacity, they still have some residual value as television material; a good film remains a good film even when it is out of date and when it has already been seen by most cinema-goers. From a television point of view it is still worth exhibiting as a good work of visual art and to show it is more likely to bring good than harm to those who make films.

The chief opposition comes, not from the makers of cinema films, but from the exhibitors—the owners of cinema houses. They have contended that, if a cinema film, however old, is available on television, people will stay at home to see it rather than go out to the cinema to see a new film. The assumption here is that the drawing power of an old cinema film is essentially greater than anything the television industry can produce for itself, but this is not true. For a long time on Saturday nights the BBC alternated old cinema films with live plays of its own production. There was no significant difference in the audience ratings; neither was noticeably more popular than the other on average.

In fact the use of cinema films for television in this country is very limited indeed—much more limited than in the United States and most other countries. Our own television industry is so productive that its need for canned products made by other people is relatively small. The British cinema industry may have been hit by television in general, but there is no evidence to suggest that it has been hit in a particular way by the televising of old films originally made for the cinema.

CHAPTER 12

Colour Television

COLOUR is broadcasting's third dimension. Colour television has been available to the public in America for eight years or more, and more recently it has been adopted in Japan and the Soviet Union, but Britain lags behind. Why do we, the people who led the world in monochrome television, find ourselves so far behind in colour?

Most of the basic research in colour was carried out in America after the war, when Britain was economically exhausted, and several systems emerged. Some systems were 'compatible' others 'incompatible'. A 'compatible' system is one which permits a colour picture to be received as a black and white picture on black and white receiving sets, while an 'incompatible' system transmits colour pictures which can only be received on colour receiving sets. For obvious reasons a compatible system is greatly preferable to an incompatible system, other things being more or less equal. When a public service of colour television in America became a practical possibility, it was necessary to choose the best system and to adopt it as the national standard for the USA. So a committee of experts was set up. It was called the National Television Systems Committee and it recommended a particular compatible system which is now known as the NTSC system. Thereupon the Radio Corporation of America went into business, and began to manufacture colour receivers for sale to the public. At the same time its broadcasting subsidiary, the National Broadcasting Company, began to transmit several hours a day of colour programmes through its network, and a rival network, the Columbia Broadcasting System, followed suit.

But all was not plain sailing. The third national network, the American Broadcasting Company did not follow, and eventually

TELEVISION: A CRITICAL REVIEW

the Columbia Broadcasting System became discouraged at the slow progress and dropped out of the colour race. The NBC remained and still remains as the sole torch-bearer of colour television in America. At the back of NBC is the most powerful radio manufacturing corporation in the world, whose board chairman, General David Sarnoff, told me eighteen months ago that his corporation had invested many millions in colour television and he was not in the least worried about the investment. He believes in the future of colour. However, colour television in America has made a disappointingly slow start. I was in America only about four months ago, and even then it had not really got properly off the ground; the highest estimate given to me was half a million colour sets in use then. A more recent figure to reach me is 700,000, a small figure for so large a potential market. The main trouble, I think, was that the early receivers were not sufficiently foolproof in the hands of ordinary people without technical understanding, but now it is judged that this particular difficulty has been largely overcome and there is no reason why colour television should not go ahead rapidly in the near future. That also is the opinion of the BBC, whose research engineers succeeded several years ago in adapting the NTSC system to British conditions. They have already spent a quarter of a million pounds in experiments, from which both the BBC and the radio manufacturers have gained important experience.

Some people have blamed the relatively high cost of colour receivers, but I do not agree. In these days of hire purchase the price seldom deters people from having what they want, if they want it badly enough. When we get into mass production in this country, we ought to be able to get good colour receivers for about £150. (In America they are about $450.) It should be remembered that the BBC had three-quarters of a million licensed viewers at a time when a 14-inch black and white receiver cost nearly £200. In my opinion the price of the receiving set is not going to be an important deterrent, provided it is really reliable.

When I was Director of BBC Television I was always most anxious to make a start in compatible colour even, if necessary, before colour sets were on the market. My reason for this was the desire to gain experience for our operational engineers and

COLOUR TELEVISION

producing staff, to stimulate the manufacturers to greater speed and to show the world and our own people that Britain was in the colour business. An hour a week for a start would have satisfied me, but I wanted it to be part of the normal publicized programme, where it would be noticed; not unpublicized experimental transmissions which incidentally have been undertaken by the BBC for years.

But unhappily colour became hopelessly entangled with the question of picture line standards. I remember one evening several years ago spent with Ernest Marples, then Postmaster General, at the Lime Grove Studios. This was long before the Pilkington Committee was even thought of. He was telling me how he hoped during his term of office as PMG to solve the twin problems of colour and line standards. I said I saw no necessary connection between the two, but he insisted there was a connection in his own mind, while I held to my view that to tie colour to the line standards problem was unrealistic and would hold colour back. We parted good friends without either having convinced the other.

Here I must explain the so-called twin problems. Every television screen consists of a number of horizontal lines, which carry the picture. They are visible as separate lines if you get near enough to the screen. The number of lines varies as between one country and another, but with the exception of Belgium which is a special case, all sets within any one country have the same number of lines. No set can receive a picture unless the picture is being transmitted on exactly the number of lines for which the set was built. The number of lines is known as the line standard. The British line standard is 405; the American is 525; the European and Soviet bloc is 625. Other things being equal, the more lines the better the quality of the picture. Thus Britain has the world's lowest standard, because we were the first, and 405 lines was the best anybody could achieve in 1936. While the BBC could change its line standard quite cheaply, the owners of the millions of receiving sets could not; they would in fact have to buy new sets, which would be unthinkable. So BBC and ITA have to go on using 405 lines until some special arrangements are made at Government level for a change over which would not inflict financial hardship on the viewers. This is the line standards problem.

It is soluble over a long period, perhaps twenty years from now. Sufficient new channels in the ultra high frequency band could be allotted to both BBC and ITA to enable both to duplicate their present networks. They would then transmit their present services in duplicate: that is to say on 625 lines and on 405 lines simultaneously. The manufacture of 405 line sets would have to be stopped after a certain date and transmissions on 405 lines would have to continue until all the 405 line sets were worn out and due for replacement. By then all receiving sets would be on 625 and both television authorities would cease transmitting on 405.

It has been argued by people who want to go slow over colour, that it would be wrong to start colour on 405 lines, when we know, or think we know, that we are going to make a change to 625 lines. The implication, I suppose, is that there would be something immoral in making and selling to the public colour receivers which can only accept 405 lines, because one day they will be out of date. But that is equally true of black and white sets; all the black and white sets which are now being made and will be made for several years to come will be on 405 lines and will be out of date when in perhaps twenty years time we cease to transmit on 405. It is no more immoral to sell a colour set which will eventually be out of date than it is to sell black and white sets, which will eventually be out of date.

Meanwhile it is just as easy for the BBC to transmit colour on 405 lines as on any other line standard; indeed it has been doing so experimentally for years with excellent results. (It is also experimenting with colour on 625 lines, with an eye to the future.) So there really is no necessary connection between colour and line standards; they are two quite distinct subjects, and it is a pity they have become confused in the public mind.

In December, 1960, the BBC made formal application to the Postmaster General for permission to start a limited non-experimental service in colour on 405 lines beginning in November, 1961. I never understood why the PMG's permission should have been necessary when we already had his permission to transmit 405 line colour experimentally. However it was probably the correct thing to do, and to my astonishment he refused permission pending the publication of the Pilkington Report. So colour television for Britain was delayed for at least another year and perhaps much longer. The Pilkington Committee can only make one of two recommendations. Either to let the BBC do what it asked to do in 1960, or to delay the introduction of colour until we are ready to transmit it on 625 lines. In the latter event colour for the whole nation will be delayed by a further six to ten years, because that is the time it will take to build the new ultra high frequency transmitting stations to radiate 625 line pictures. The latter course would be folly; instead of being fourth in the colour race, which is the best we can hope for now, Britain might be tenth or even twentieth.

Quite apart from whether the British people want colour or not—and I believe most of them will when they see it—the opportunities it will provide for exports, especially if we go into the Common Market, will be most important. It seems a great pity to me that the country has been so slow and unenterprising in a field where its past record for enterprise has been second to none.

Until about a year ago the BBC seemed to be fighting a lone battle for colour television; it seemed to be a case of public enterprise versus private unenterprise, but in the last twelve months or so there has been a welcome change for the better. In the late summer of 1961 the BBC was permitted for the first time to mount a comprehensive demonstration of colour at the annual National Radio Exhibition at Olympia. In previous years the Radio Industries Council had objected to public demonstrations of colour, because their members were not ready to satisfy a demand for colour receivers. Now it is reported that several of the members are prepared to put colour receivers on the market within two years of the authorization of a colour service on 405 lines. ITA and some of its contractors are coming to life too. It is reported that one contracting company, ABC, intends to do colour experiments using a new French system, which has had a certain amount of publicity lately. Another, Television Wales and West, gave a public demonstratiton of colour on closed circuit at the recent Bath and West Show at Taunton. All this is encouraging and it suggests that colour may after all be just round the corner.

In matters of this sort the BBC is only one of four parties. It cannot go ahead without the other three, which are the manufacturers of receivers, the ITA and the Government. The two first are showing signs of willingness. The Government is waiting for Pilkington.

CHAPTER 13

Pay TV

THE most interesting and revolutionary development on the horizon is 'Pay Television'. It would seem at first thought to offer a real solution to most of television's more serious handicaps, because it could free the medium both from dependence on government collected licence money and from the straightjacket of advertising contracts. It could put television for the first time into a normal relationship with its customers, supplying programmes in return for specific payments.

Pay TV is a system involving the transmission of programmes on to which the supplier has imposed a deliberate technical fault. The fault distorts the picture and the accompanying sound so badly that the programme is useless to the viewer unless he is in a position to correct the fault. The viewer is provided by the supplier with a piece of apparatus, which on payment of the appropriate fee, either in cash or on credit, corrects the fault and enables the viewer to enjoy the particular programme, for which he has paid. The piece of apparatus is therefore a box office—something which broadcasting has always lacked. The distortion process is known as 'Scrambling'; the correcting process as 'Unscrambling'.

This conjures up visions of no more licence fees, no more advertising, everything a straightforward deal between the supplier and the customers, with no intermediaries demanding their rake-off and no interference from other interested parties. It suggests a system by which owners of rights, whether they be promoters, producers, performers or writers could get paid in precise proportion to the financial success of their programmes. Everybody would know exactly what a programme was worth, because the unscrambling boxes would automatically record the takings; everybody could be paid a percentage of what was in the boxes, according to some prearranged 'share out'. The viewer would benefit too, because he would pay only for those programmes which he had chosen to view and not for any others; he would be in the same position as a patron of a theatre or cinema, free to choose his programmes or to stay away if he wants to.

Pay TV depends primarily on the efficiency of that little box and of course on its defence against the technically-minded cracksman. For years designers in America have been working on it; they have produced several models—Telemeter, Zenith, Skiatron are names well-known to us in the business, and more recently the Marconi Company over here has announced yet another box of their own design. The only one I know from personal experience is the American Telemeter, which is the property of the International Telemeter Corporation, a wholly owned subsidiary of the Paramount Picture Corporation. The President of the Telemeter Corporation is an old friend of several years' standing. He and I have had many meetings and conversations about Pay TV, and by his kindness I have seen demonstrations of Telemeter both in New York and in London. It is a most ingenious contraption, quite small, inoffensive in appearance and apparently designed to meet every possible eventuality including giving you credit for any surplus money you have put in the slot. It is not a credit system, like some of the others; it is a coin box system; it records what programmes have been unscrambled, and these should correspond with the money in the box, which is inspected and emptied periodically by a visiting meter reader. It deals with three television programmes simultaneously, thus providing a wide field of choice, and in addition it has a looped sound circuit, which you can turn on at any time to hear what programmes are on offer and how much you have to pay to have them unscrambled. I have no doubt the other systems are equally ingenious, but not having seen them, I am not in a position to describe them.

Never before has it been possible to take payment from the public for individual programmes. We have always had to accept bulk payment overtly through the licence system or covertly through the price of consumer goods, but now, it seems, the television box office has arrived. It has never been used except experimentally and on a very limited scale. Its use in America has been held back by all kinds of interests, though the Federal Communications Commission seems to favour proper experiments. In Britain it is, like most other things, awaiting the Pilkington Report and the decisions which must follow. The best experiment so far has been going on for about two years in Etobicoke, a suburb of Toronto, where Telemeter has been installed in 6,000 homes, to which three programmes are fed simultaneously on closed circuit. Programme A carries new feature films, B carries older ones. Presumably the charges for A are higher than for B. C, which consists of local material of various kinds and news, is mostly free. Each film is played twice nightly for several consecutive nights. It is clear that in this experiment Pay TV is being used mainly as a home cinema, but there is no physical reason to prevent it being used for a live television service, if the number of viewing homes were large enough to support it.

Etobicoke is a prosperous residential area with large blocks of flats, which lend themselves to economical working of a closed circuit installation, and it has good reception by ordinary methods of several Canadian and some American television stations. The results of the experiment so far seem to have been disappointing. Each box must attract a certain minimum of custom to cover the overheads of installation, collection and management. Reports suggest that the use of the boxes is below what it should be to make the system viable, but it does not necessarily follow from this limited experiment that Pay TV will never be viable.

The size of the takings per box per week necessary to make closed circuit Pay TV viable is still largely a matter of guesswork; the Americans seem to think $2 a week average is the minimum, while in this country 15s. is being mentioned—roughly £40 a year. Let us compare this figure with the prices of the BBC and ITA services. The former demands £2 a year from every household with television, the latter an average of about £6 a year from every household with or without television; Pay TV would demand at least another £40 a year. For one reason or the other every viewing household in Britain is compelled to pay the £2 and the £6, but there is no compulsion to pay the £40. It will be paid only if the Pay TV service can be made so much more attractive than the other two that people in large numbers will wish to pay the extra £40 to get it. In short the competitive cards are stacked very heavily against Pay TV.

It is perhaps unfortunate for Pay TV that it has arrived at so late a stage, when television broadcasting is already firmly established and powerful. If it had arrived twenty years ago, it is conceivable that we might have established it as the only permissible method of distributing and financing television programmes in Britain, and that would have saved a lot of trouble and solved many problems. The high price would have made development slower, but the absence of competition from television broadcasting would have given Pay TV a far better chance than it has today.

However, there are people in this country who seem to believe that Pay TV has something unique to offer, which will be so compelling as to induce large numbers of people to pay the extra £40 a year over and above what they must pay anyway for the two existing services. A number of companies have already been registered. Not being in touch with them, I do not know what they have in mind, but I cannot think of enough unique programme material, not already available on BBC or ITA, which would justify so high a price to the viewer. Admittedly there are some things not available to normal television broadcasting, and they all have one element in common. Their promoters want to sell them at the highest possible price for the smallest possible exposure. Professional boxing championships are a case in point. The promoters judge that televising them would damage their box office takings, because everybody could see the fight at home. The same would apply to current theatrical productions televised in full. Above all it would apply to films made at tremendous cost for showing in cinemas; these films must recover their costs and make their profits through the cinema box office before they are exposed to the millions on television. In these three categories normal television broadcasting could never pay the price necessary to compensate the promoters for the box office losses they think they would sustain, but Pay TV could. If Pay TV were successful the compensation would be so large that on purely financial grounds the local box office wouldn't matter, and if Pay TV were not so successful the exposure would be too small to affect the box office in any material way. So, successful or not, Pay TV is likely to be more attractive than television broadcasting to the promoters of exceptionally popular and expensive shows, and these things, now denied to television broadcasting, might find their way on to the Pay TV screen. But, apart from cinema films, the quantity of such things is so lamentably small that it could not begin to provide the basis of a service to the public for which they would be expected to pay £40 a year.

Cinema films may provide the answer. The people who are most enthusiastic about Pay TV are the people who have interests in film production. The Telemeter Corporation for instance is a wholly owned subsidiary of the Paramount Picture Corporation. Hundreds of cinemas, especially in Britain and America, are being closed every year because of the competition of television broadcasting. In other words the exhibitors of cinema films are packing up, but the makers of cinema films are very much alive, with no intention of packing up; they are looking for a new kind of exhibitor to take the place of the old one. They need another kind of box office, and Pay TV can provide it right in the home. As a home cinema, a domestic extension of the local movie theatre, it might be very successful indeed. One could see the film in one's armchair without having to go out of doors; it would be so easy and comfortable and convenient, and probably less expensive than buying the better seats in the cinema. Then there is the family to be thought of; one would not have to pay for them too; they could just sit around at home and see it without any expense at all.

There is another school of thought favourable to Pay TV, the people whose capacity for appreciation, both intellectual and artistic, is beyond average. They are the kind of people for whom the Third Programme in radio is provided, and they find that television in its present form does not, except on rather rare occasions, satisfy this side of their natures. It is not sufficiently esoteric, because its dependence on big audiences prevents it from paying much attention to the specialized requirements of very small audiences. They believe they see in Pay TV an escape from this situation. Some part of a Pay TV service could, it is argued, be given up to material of this sort on a regular basis, and the fact that the audience would be a small one would not matter, because it would be a paying audience large enough to cover the costs of the programmes. The object these people have in mind is admirable, and I wish it could be achieved somehow, but I do not expect it to happen in Pay TV. The colossal investment necessary to establish a nation-wide Pay TV service, the overhead costs of running it and the inevitable losses in the first few years would force the Pay TV authority to concentrate on programme material of the widest popular appeal. To make themselves viable they would need millions of customers putting on average £40 a year into each box. The struggle for the mass audience would be as fierce as in competitive commercial television. I cannot see how they could, at any rate for many years, afford the luxury of a regular service of this kind at a convenient time of day, however much they might wish, on other grounds, to do it. The best hope of satisfying this particular requirement, perhaps only partially, is the BBC's second network.

While in no sense unsympathetic towards Pay TV, I have pointed to what I believe to be its weaknesses. I have suggested that, as a box office for the cinema film industry, it could be valuable, and I should like to see it used on a local closed circuit basis for that purpose, but as a box office for television broadcasting it has come too late. In some ways I regret it, but it seems to me that by now most of the cards are stacked against it. I may be too pessimistic, and it may be that Pay TV's one strong card will prove stronger than I expect.

The card is this. Owners of rights in exceptionally popular shows, whether they be their own performances or writings, whether they be contests or events they are promoting, prefer to put a fence round themselves. They like to admit into the enclosure only those who are willing to pay the price, and the rest they prefer to exclude. Television broadcasting cannot offer them these conditions, but Pay TV could. The scrambling of the programme is the equivalent of the fence; the payment and the unscrambling is the equivalent of the turnstile. Having put your money into the box you are inside; otherwise you are out. To the owner of an exceptionally popular spectacle or performance this could be a very attractive proposition, and, because it is an attribute of Pay TV and not of television broadcasting, it could put the former into a more favourable bargaining position. This to my mind is Pay TV's only strong card. There are certain events and certain people, not very numerous admittedly, that nearly everybody wants to see or hear, and if the home viewer can't get them on the ordinary television, he might well be willing to pay a few extra shillings to have them on Pay TV. If millions did this, the financial rewards for the promoters and performers would be enormous.

Television broadcasters everywhere are apprehensive of Pay TV's potential bargaining strength. It must be remembered that this strength would apply to only very few events and personalities, but they would be the cream so far as popular appeal is concerned. It seems that Pay TV, in addition to showing material not now available on television broadcasting, might be able to skim the cream off what is now available to the millions. No doubt this would be the rough and tumble of normal business competition, if television were free private enterprise, but, as I have stated elsewhere in this book, television is neither free nor private. It is fully within the realm of public policy, and those who decide public policy may have to make up their minds whether the few exceptionally popular programmes now available to households paying about £8 a year shall be withdrawn and made the exclusive privilege of those who can afford an extra £40 a year.

It would, of course, be a great mistake to imagine that any television service can live on cream; there isn't enough of it, and if there were more it would be less valuable. The vast bulk of television programming is of a wholly different nature, in which Pay TV would have no special advantage and one very big disadvantage (price) over its competitors.

My own attitude towards Pay TV has always been agnostic. I have discussed it with some of the leading people in American television. The most common attitude appears to be something like this—'We don't expect it to impinge much on television broadcasting, but if it does we shall get into it ourselves'. In America there is a strong broadcasting lobby against it, based I think on a vague fear that it might be dangerous to established interests. David Sarnoff, Board Chairman of RCA, gave me an astronomical figure as the probable capital investment necessary to get a nation-wide Pay TV service going. The figure was so high as to make it virtually out of the question.

There are two approaches to a Pay TV network. One approach

assumes that the programmes would be radiated through broadcasting transmitters in their scrambled form; the other assumes closed circuit transmission through cables. The former method would require a much more complex and expensive unscrambling box in the viewing home than the latter, and the average takings per box would need to be correspondingly higher. Closed circuit would seem to be a better business proposition.

The reader may be asking what is the essential difference between closed circuit Pay TV and the many local closed circuit systems, which already exist for supplying BBC and ITA programmes into the home. The answer is that the existing systems offer convenient reception facilities on a rental basis and nothing else; no part of the rental goes towards the cost of the programmes; no box office is involved. (I presume that the existing systems could be used in conjunction with Pay TV, but that is another matter.)

Here I am going to risk a forecast. I do not expect Pay TV to be widely used in the foreseeable future as a box office for the television industry, but it could become a box office in the home for the film industry.

CHAPTER 14

Into the Future

SINCE writing this book Telstar has gone into orbit, the Pilkington Committee has presented a report, which shows a depth of understanding hitherto unrivalled in broadcasting literature; the Government has produced a White Paper on its immediate intentions, and debates have taken place in both Houses of Parliament. The terms of reference of the Pilkington Committee permitted it to recommend more but not less competition; the continued existence of the BBC and the ITA as separate entities was postulated in advance, and so there was to remain the familiar element of competition between these two dissimilar authorities, which the committee had to accept.

They found, as they were bound to find, an incompatibility of motive between good broadcasting and profitable TV advertising, and so they recommend that the advertising function be transferred from the contracting companies, which have a profit motive, to the ITA which has no profit motive. The transfer would be unworkable unless the function of programme planning were transferred at the same time; so this is recommended too. Two commercial networks under the ITA are envisaged, but because both will be members of one family they will not be in full competition with each other, and the worst evils of competitive commercial television will be avoided.

The 'Programme Companies' will become programme companies, making programmes for sale to the ITA, the BBC and any other exhibitor of television material, at home or abroad, who may be willing to buy them. The profitability of their businesses will not depend on audience ratings but on the acceptability of their products to the networks to which they are offered; and these networks, it is hoped, will only want material which is compatible with a policy of well-balanced programming.

As this is in line with the policy of the BBC we should have two authorities, each controlling a pair of complementary networks, competing with each other, not primarily for mass audiences, but for good broadcasting. I can find no fault with this objective, and if it can be achieved it will be wholly beneficial.

But there remains a moral obligation to the programme companies, who were induced by the Television Act of 1954 to enter the television business, and so ITA must guarantee a large volume of business for them, because in practice ITA will be almost their only customer. This in turn will limit the ITA's freedom to build up its own production resources and to go shopping in the world's programme market. It is difficult for me to envisage a television authority, fully responsible for its programme services as ITA would be, yet tied by long-term contracts for the supply of most of its programmes. It might work out satisfactorily, but my experience has taught me how valuable it is to be free of such commitments, if the best results are to be obtained. Perhaps, before this volume is published, the Government will have reached a decision on this difficult point.

The BBC's future is much clearer; most of the Pilkington recommendations have been accepted, and the Government undertakes to insure that adequate financial provision will be made for the BBC's authorized developments, which include colour and a second television network. But I detect a lack of firmness over the licence revenue, which disturbs me. Britain has almost the lowest licence charge in the world, and a proper increase would not be unacceptable to our people; they might grumble at first, but they would pay and they would know they were getting good value. There is no other way of increasing the BBC's revenue except a government subsidy, which would be immensely damaging and would destroy the unique status of British broadcasting at home and abroad. The suggestion that part of the surpluses from ITA's advertising operations might be applied to BBC development is disingenuous in the extreme; a subsidy is a subsidy no matter where the Government gets the money from, and a subsidy opens the door to government control of broadcasting, which, if it ever came, would undermine the work of forty years.

The Pilkington Report says, 'Only the licence fee system implies no commitment to any objective other than the provision of the best possible service of broadcasting,' and in a later paragraph, '... it is clear that the BBC's service in the United Kingdom is cheaper today, and for the most part very much cheaper, than services similarly financed in Western European countries.' Referring to the proposed increase in the licence fee and the additional services that will be financed by it the report says, '... 4d. a day is remarkably little as a household expense,' and paragraph 506 reads as follows: 'We are convinced that financing the BBC out of licence revenue, and only out of licence revenue, is more than an important feature of the Corporation's constitution. The BBC sees it as essential. We see it as essential. For the BBC must remain free of any commitment, express or implied, to pursue any objective whatsoever other than the full realization of the purposes of broadcasting.'

The Pilkington Committee have performed a number of very important functions. Firstly they have advised the Government and Parliament how to deal in the next twelve years with a complex situation made more difficult by the mistake of the Television Act of 1954. I confess that, when I first heard their proposals for reforming commercial television, I was surprised at the lengths to which they had gone. They were precluded by their terms of reference from recommending its complete abolition, and, this being so, I had expected them to accept, *faut de mieux*, the dominance of the Programme Companies. But further thought and careful study of the report have convinced me that if commercial television is to be a constructive and more or less permanent feature of British life, it must be controlled by a public corporation not primarily interested in profits. The ITA is such a corporation, but, lacking nearly all the attributes of a broadcasting authority, it is not in fact in control. The Committee recommend that it should be given those attributes, which are financial control, editorial control and some machinery for creative production. None of these except the last can be given to the ITA without taking them completely away from the programme companies, which is what the Committee recommend. The surplus revenue from the advertising operation will go into the public purse instead of into the pockets of private shareholders, who have come to regard these shares as money for jam. Pressure from the shareholders and those who represent them will be the Government's most formidable obstacle in carrying out the Pilkington recommendations.

The Committee have performed another function of even more lasting value, and in my opinion of world-wide importance. They have defined the 'Purposes of Broadcasting' in terms combining wisdom with practical understanding, which could be applied to broadcasting in any country. It should no longer be possible with any degree of plausibility for people to pretend that there are two alternative philosophies of broadcasting; to give the public what it wants or to give the public what someone thinks is good for it. No competent professional broadcaster subscribes to either, and the myth that they exist in mutual conflict within the broadcasting industry is the illusion of non-professional persons who hope to make easy money by employing professionals to 'give the public what it wants'. In the Committee's view both attitudes, if they were to exist, would be patronizing and arrogant. In fact neither was expressed in evidence to the Committee by the BBC, the ITA, or the programme companies, and it is encouraging to know that professional opinion in all branches of the broadcasting industry is more mature and responsible than some spokesmen would lead us to suppose.

Paragraph 46 of the report expresses what I believe to be the faith of all mature broadcasters not only in Britain but in Europe, the Commonwealth and the United States too: 'No one can say he is giving the public what it wants, unless the public knows the whole range of possibilities which television can offer and, from this range, chooses what it wants to see. For a choice is only free if the field of choice is not unnecessarily restricted. The subject matter of television is to be found in the whole scope and variety of human awareness and experience. If viewers—"the public"—are thought of as "the mass audience" or "the majority", they will be shown only the average of common experience and awareness; the "ordinary"; the commonplace—for what all know and do is, by definition, commonplace. They will be kept unaware of what lies beyond the average of experience; their field of choice will be limited. In time they may come to like only what they know. But it will always be true that, had they been offered a wider range from which to

INTO THE FUTURE

choose, they might and often would have chosen otherwise, and with greater enjoyment.'

That the professionals should be given wide scope and kept free from the inhibitions of governmental and commercial interests is the principal theme of the Pilkington Report.

I was glad to find support for my belief that *competitive* commercial television is the worst evil. A memorandum submitted to the committee on behalf of my old friend, the late Sir Richard Boyer, for many years Chairman of the Australian Broadcasting Commission, contains these sentences: 'Indeed it is very much to the credit of the programme companies operating under the ITA that they have so far given prominence to the informative and educational side of television. At present, however, these companies have no commercial competitors. It is when direct commercial competition enters the field that these services to the community are apt to be relegated to the "off peak" hours in favour of the high-audience ratings which most concern advertisers'. And 'In fact the diversity of programmes tends to decline as commercial competition increases.' Thus Sir Richard Boyer, from his wide experience in another country, reinforces my conviction that the worst menace comes, not from commercial television *per se* but from competitive commercial television.

The committee's views on Educational Broadcasting are thoroughly sound. They reject the ITA's plea for a specialized educational network, using much the same arguments as I have used in my chapter 'Education and Instruction'. Preferring comprehensive networks they say 'As one of the major purposes of television, education must be defined in its most liberal sense: as the development of the imagination, of the spirit of enquiry, of the critical attitude; as promoting breadth of interest and understanding; as making for the greatest awareness of the possibilities of mind and feeling open to human experience; in summary as an essential part of the purpose of a full life.'

When dealing with instructional television the report says 'How best to make good the shortage of teachers is, of course, essentially a problem of educational rather than broadcasting policy'. But they do not draw to the attention of the educational authorities, particularly the universities, the exciting possibilities of teaching by electronic methods on closed circuit. As this is not a broadcasting matter it presumably lay outside the scope of the committee's work.

On the whole the prospects for British broadcasting are better now than they have been for many years; there is a truer understanding of its purposes and of its vulnerability to misuse by those who would have it as a private source of easy money or political influence. There is a growing realization that public channels of communication must be used in the public interest, and that honest communication between men of all social, political and racial groups must be enlarged and enriched if the human race is to keep pace with its own prolific ingenuity. We live in an age of ideological conflict in which two giants compete for world leadership, with rigid adherence to outworn but diametrically opposed political philosophies; the totalitarian state competes with the state which is not even allowed by Congress to regulate broadcasting in the public interest.

Against this background the flexibility of the British is impressive and nowhere is it better illustrated than in broadcasting. No ideology keeps us from state regulation of the things which are public, nor from state protection of the things which are private. For many reasons, historical, geographical and temperamental, it is easier for us to assimilate broadcasting, holding it to its more fruitful uses, and avoiding the extremes of political and commercial exploitation; yet ten years ago it seemed that our understanding of these things was waning. Perhaps the poverty and hardship of war and war's aftermath caused too many of our people to equate the good with the profitable, and we nearly threw away one of our great heirlooms, because of the softening of a political party, which up to then had stood firmly for high standards in broadcasting. It is impossible to forecast the actions of governments. This one, through a desire to conciliate established interests, may at first do less than is needed to put television back on its true course, but there is no longer any doubt about the direction in which the course lies.

INDEX

ABC, 135
Abercorn, Duke of, 23
Adam, Kenneth, 33, 78, 99, 100
Adorian, Paul, 129
Aga Khan, the, 35
Alexandra Palace, 39
All India Radio, 25
American Broadcasting Company, 131
Ampex, 126
'Any Questions', 31
ARTV, 129
Ashbridge, Noel, 17
ATV, 124
Australia, 90, 149

Baird System, 39
Baldwin, Stanley, 23
Barnes, George, 32, 33, 42, 78
Bath and West Show, 135
BBC Concerts Committee, 25
BBC Economy Committee, 31
BBC Symphony Orchestra, 25, 28
Beadle, Charles, 9, 10
Beadle, Clayton, 11
Beadle, Frank, 12
Beard, Paul, 28
Birkinshaw, Douglas, 40
Bishop, Harold, 17, 40
Blumlein, Allan, 41
Boult, Adrian, 25, 28
Boyer, Richard, 149
Brandies, Justice, 50
Briggs, Asa, 68
British Broadcasting Company Ltd, 15, 16
Brown, Cecil, 41
Burgess, Guy, 27
Burrows, Arthur, 17

Cable Film, 113, 114
Canada, 36, 55, 90
Carpendale, Charles, 18, 19, 38
Cawston, Richard, 121
Central Council for School Broadcasting, 101
'Choice', 86
Clarke, Douglas, 24
Cock, Gerald, 33, 38, 39, 40, 41
Collins, Norman, 41, 78
Columbia Broadcasting System, 41, 49, 117, 131, 132
Committee of Public Accounts, 56, 57, 61
Cone, Fairfax, 90, 91

Coronation 1937, 39
Craigavon, Lord, 23
Cruft, Eugene, 28
Cup Finals, 40
Davis, John, 128
Derby, the, 40
Durban, 20, 21
'Durban Calling', 21

Eckersley, Peter, 16, 23
Eckersley, Roger, 23, 24
Eden, Anthony, 35, 67
Education, Ministry of, 101
EMI Ltd, 39
Emitron, 41
Empire Broadcasting Service, 24
Epilogue, the, 26
Etobicoke, 139
European Broadcasting Union, 109
Eurovision, 109, 110, 111, 112

Federal Communications Commission, 47, 49, 95, 139
Foot, Robert, 29, 30
Ford Foundation, the, 102
Foreign policy, 43
Foreign programmes, 108
France, 36, 46, 50, 108

Gaitskell, Hugh, 67
General Strike 1926, 29, 68
Gillard, Frank, 30
Gorham, Maurice, 33, 41
Graves, Cecil, 24, 30
Greene, Hugh Carleton, 31, 35
'Gresham's Law', 79, 80
Grisewood, Freddy, 19

Haley, William, 24, 30, 31, 32, 34, 41, 78
Harding, Archie, 26
Harty, Hamilton, 25
Hibberd, Stewart, 19
Home Guard, 28

Iconoscope, 41
Imperial Airways, 27
Intervision, 112, 113
Iremonger, Freddy, 26
Italy, 36, 106

Jacob, Ian, 34, 40, 59, 79, 128
Janot, Mons, 68

Kinescope, 126
Kipping, Norman, 127

Lever Bros., 13
Lewis, Cecil, 17
Licence Revenue, 56, 57, 58, 59, 84
London Concerts Committee, 25
Lotbiniere, Seymour de, 33

Madden, Cecil, 40
Magnet House, 15
Marconi House, 15
Marples, Ernest, 133
MGM, 124
Midwest Program on Airborne Television Instruction, 101, 102
Minow, Newton, 47, 48, 49, 50, 51
Monoply, 70 et seq., 87, 88
Murrow, Edward R., 117
Music Corporation of America, 122, 123

McCulloch, Derek, 28
McGivern, Cecil, 78

National Association of Broadcasters, 48
National Broadcasting Company of America, 41, 49, 113, 117, 131, 132
National Radio Exhibition, 135
National Television Systems Committee, 131
New Zealand, 90
Nicolls, Basil, 30
Nixon, Vice-President Richard, 35
Northern Ireland, 22, 23, 24

Ogilvie, Frederick, 28, 29
Olympia, 135

Paley, William, 41
Parliament, 34, 35
Pears, Andrew, 9, 10
Pilkington Committee, 134, 135, 136, 139, 145, 146, 147
Proms, the, 25
Pulling, Martin, 33
Purdue University, 102

Radio Corporation of America, 41, 131
Radio Industries Council, 135
Radio Manufacturers' Association, 41
Radio Olympia, 39
Radio Times, 19, 23
Rank Organization, 128

Reissini, Nicolas, 129
Reith, John, 14, 15, 17, 18, 20, 22, 23, 24, 26, 27, 28, 37, 41, 68, 72
Religious Broadcasting, 25
RKO, 129
Roberts, John, 20
Robin International, 129
Royal Family, 35

Sarnoff, David, 41, 132, 143
Sarnoff, Robert, 49
Savoy Hill, 15, 16
Schoenberg, Isaac, 41
Schuster, Leonard, 40
Seipman, Charles, 24
Shields, Isobel, 13, 14, 16
Snagge, John, 19
South African Broadcasting Corporation, 22
Staff Training School, 26, 27, 103
Stanley, C. O., 41
Stanton, Frank, 49, 50, 51
Stobart, J. C., 25, 26
Suez, 67

Taylor, H. Lyall, 21
Telemeter, 138, 139
Telerecording, 126
Television Act 1954, 34
Television Centre, 125
Television Licence, 60
Telstar, 113, 114, 145
Third Programme, 95, 98
Thomson, Roy, 44
Treasury, the, 57, 58, 59, 60
TWW, 135
Tudsbery, M. T., 39

United States, 36, 43, 46, 47
USSR, 107

Video Tape Recording, 126

Waldman, Ronald, 33
War, outbreak of, 28, 40
Wellington, Lindsay, 24
West Region, 27
White City, 32
Williams, Stuart, 33
Wilson, Professor H. H., 81, 82
Wood, Henry, 25
Wynn, Rowland, 17

Zworykin, Vladimir, 41

For Product Safety Concerns and Information please contact our EU
representative GPSR@taylorandfrancis.com
Taylor & Francis Verlag GmbH, Kaufingerstraße 24, 80331 München, Germany

www.ingramcontent.com/pod-product-compliance
Lightning Source LLC
Chambersburg PA
CBHW061452300426
44114CB00014B/1945